BRIEF THERAPY
WITH COUPLES

WILEY SERIES
in
BRIEF THERAPY AND COUNSELLING

Editor
Windy Dryden

Brief Rational Emotive Behaviour Therapy
Windy Dryden

Brief Therapeutic Consultations
An approach to systemic counselling
Eddy Street and Jim Downey

Brief Therapy with Couples
An integrative approach
Maria Gilbert and Diana Shmukler

Further titles in preparation

BRIEF THERAPY WITH COUPLES

An integrative approach

Maria Gilbert and Diana Shmukler

JOHN WILEY & SONS

Chichester · New York · Brisbane · Toronto · Singapore

Copyright © 1996 by John Wiley & Sons Ltd,
Baffins Lane, Chichester,
West Sussex PO19 1UD, England

National   01243 779777
International   (+44) 1243 779777
e-mail (for orders and customer service enquiries):
cs-books@wiley.co.uk
Visit our Home Page on http://www.wiley.co.uk
or http://www.wiley.com

Other Wiley Editorial Offices

John Wiley & Sons, Inc., 605 Third Avenue,
New York, NY 10158-0012, USA

Jacaranda Wiley Ltd, 33 Park Road, Milton,
Queensland 4064, Australia

John Wiley & Sons (Canada) Ltd, 22 Worcester Road,
Rexdale, Ontario M9W 1L1, Canada

John Wiley & Sons (Asia) Pte Ltd, 2 Clementi Loop #02-01,
Jin Xing Distripark, Singapore 129809

Library of Congress Cataloging-in-Publication Data

Gilbert, Maria
    Brief therapy with couples/Maria Gilbert & Diana Shmukler.
        p.   cm.—(Wiley series in brief therapy and counselling)
    Includes bibliographical references and index.
    ISBN 0-471-96206-6
    1. Marital psychotherapy. 2. Brief psychotherapy. I. Shmukler,
Diana. II. Title. III. Series.
RC488.5.G527   1996
616.89'156—dc20   96-33200
                                                           CIP

British Library Cataloguing in Publication Data

A catalogue record for this book is available from the British Library

ISBN 0-471-96206-6

Typeset in 10/12pt Palatino from the author's disks by
Dorwyn Ltd, Rowlands Castle, Hants
Printed and bound in Great Britain by Biddles Ltd, Guildford and Kings Lynn
This book is printed on acid-free paper responsibly manufactured from sustainable
forestation, for which at least two trees are planted for each one used for paper production.

CONTENTS

ABOUT THE AUTHORS

Maria Gilbert was brought up in South Africa where she graduated in psychology and qualified in clinical psychology. She worked for many years in private practice as a clinical psychologist and psychotherapist, and after moving to London, she was also Director of Clinical Training at Metanoia Institute, West London. Maria has extensive experience of working with couples and has trained and supervised couples therapists. She is currently head of Integrative Psychotherapy Training at Metanoia Institute.

Diana Shmukler was an Associate Professor and Head of Applied Psychology at the University of the Witwatersrand, South Africa. She is currently the Head of Integrative Psychotherapy Training at Sherwood Psychotherapy Training Institute in Nottingham. In addition to a commitment to wide-ranging research, she has interests in developmental psychology, post-traumatic stress and cultural disadvantage. Currently she is training and supervising psychotherapists in the UK, Europe and South Africa. Diana is registered as an integrative psychotherapist with the United Kingdom Council for Psychotherapy.

SERIES PREFACE

In recent years, the field of counselling and psychotherapy has become preoccupied with brief forms of intervention. While some of this interest has been motivated by expediency – reducing the amount of help that is offered to clients to make the best use of diminishing resources – there has also developed the view that brief therapy may be the treatment of choice for many people seeking therapeutic help. It is with the latter view in mind that the Wiley Series in Brief Therapy and Counselling was developed.

This series of practical texts considers different forms of brief therapy and counselling as they are practised in different settings and with different client groups. While no book can substitute for vigorous training and supervision, the purpose of the books in the present series is to provide clear guides for the practice of brief therapy and counselling, which is here defined as lasting 25 sessions or less.

Windy Dryden
Series Editor

INTRODUCTION

Our orientation and value system could be characterized as humanistic/existential in that we believe in people's inherent thrust towards growth and health. While we accept that damage and trauma leave people with deep emotional scars, much problem behaviour and acting-out we see as attempts to find solutions to pain and distress. Further we have a developmental perspective, in that we understand that unresolved problems early in life get re-enacted and re-created, usually unconsciously in adult relationships. It is particularly the dyadic constellation that re-evokes early and often primitive relatedness, in the sense that couples act out with each other issues from the past. We see this acting-out as an attempt to rectify and correct, in the present, situations that they were unable to manage in the past. That the solutions are often inappropriate is a testimony to the early and childlike nature of the needs being expressed and of the rigid repetitive strategies that were developed in response to the demands of a particular family constellation. A person's repertoire of responses will necessarily be shaped by prior experience; the more limiting and narrow the range of relationship options that a person learns, the more inflexible such a person may be in a subsequent partnership. We see our task as assisting people to broaden their range of options and to become flexible in their responses.

STAGES OF RELATIONSHIP OVER THE LIFE-SPAN

With the greater flexibility and social acceptance both around divorce and around sharing a home (without being married), people feel less constrained to stay in partnerships that are no longer satisfactory or to formalise their relationship automatically from the outset. There is also a gradual change in attitudes towards the institution of marriage, which no longer appears to be considered a requisite for people who are setting up home together. Whether two people choose to get married (in law and/or in religion) may be determined by factors such as whether they decide to have children or not, financial considerations related to issues such as tax or house ownership and religious, cultural or familial loyalties. This change in social mores has brought along with it unique problems for the couples therapist. Nowadays, dealing with remarried couples is a common occurrence as is undertaking therapy with a couple who choose to live in partnership, but do not wish to get married. It is also not unusual to deal with two people who are married while choosing to retain their own separate homes or with married partners where an 'open marriage' is under discussion.

For us as couples therapists it is emerging as an interesting, challenging and sometimes disturbing social phenomenon, that many people now have at least three primary relationships over a lifetime. In our work with couples we have regularly worked with people at different life stages. In this process, certain distinct and recognizable separate relationships have emerged. For some people all three of these 'marriages' are with the same person; for many there will be two or three partners in a lifetime.

The Relationship of Discovery: the Early Years

This relationship usually occurs in adolescence and early adulthood and involves a voyage of discovery into sexual intimacy, romantic love and being close to another person outside of the family of origin. In some cases, a person may conduct this relationship on a fantasy level, supported by movies, TV programmes and magazines. However this relationship occurs, whether in fantasy or reality, it provides the opportunity to discover and explore. If people get married young, this may be motivated by 'wanting to get away from home'.

The Relationship of the Family: the Middle Years

In adulthood (in their twenties and thirties), people choose the partner with whom they have children. This may be the same as the earlier adolescent romantic companion, but it is often a later choice. In this relationship, partners create a home for their children and are concerned with raising and educating their children, while consolidating their own careers. There is very much the sense of 'family' in this relationship. If people remarry at this stage, two families of young children may be joined in a larger family constellation by this move. This is a fairly frequent phenomenon presenting to the couples therapist.

The Relationship of Companionship: the Later Years

At this stage, the children are fully or almost fully grown, and partners look to one another for companionship. Although this may be with the previous partner, in our experience it is not unusual for people to establish a relationship with a new partner in their mid-forties or early fifties that focuses on companionship and shared interests. The death of a previous partner or a divorce may precede this stage. Alternatively, they may feel that they have 'outgrown' the previous partner or that they have 'grown apart'. The person of their choice may well be someone that they have met in a work setting and shared common interests and pursuits with as a consequence of their frequent daily contacts.

The brief-term couples therapist will be dealing with couples at any of these stages, though generally it is the second and third relationship stage that presents most frequently for therapy.

FORMAT OF THE BOOK

In this book we have described an integrative approach to brief therapy with couples based in a theory that assumes the primacy of relationship in people's lives. In Chapters 1 and 2, we discuss the aims, the advantages and the limitations of this approach to couples work. Chapter 3 gives an outline of the theoretical model that underpins our approach and draws on material from object relations, self-psychology, developmental research, transactional analysis, gestalt therapy and cognitive–analytic sources. Our intention was to integrate material from these approaches into a model for brief therapy for couples. In Chapters 4 and 5 we discuss the important elements of assessment and contracting in brief therapy with couples. Chapters 6 to 9 outline how we understand and work with the different relationship dimensions in which the primary relationship deficit occurs.

Chapter 10 is on termination and endings, Chapter 11 on the unique ethical issues related to brief therapy with couples and Chapter 12 on the supervision of brief therapy of this kind. We have chosen to use the term 'relationship' to cover all partnerships, since our work applies to married and unmarried partners, to same-sex partners and to people who choose to live apart. The term 'marriage therapy' or for 'married couples' may have been misleading to the reader, since our brief is wider than this, and these terms may have suggested a narrower focus than the one we have taken in this book. We have chosen to use 'he' and 'she' in different places to indicate that a male or a female may be referred to in these places. Where gender is significant to the subject under discussion, of course, we have made this clear in the text.

We have used pseudonyms for all our case examples and for the case study at the end. Any examples have also been substantially disguised to protect our present and past clients. Where necessary we have obtained the clients' permission.

1

DEFINITION, AIMS AND SCOPE OF BRIEF THERAPY WITH COUPLES

Brief therapy with couples as presented in this book refers to a focused six to eight session intervention with the specific aim of interrupting and redirecting repetitive outmoded patterns of communication in couples relationships. Such brief focused therapy is process-oriented; it aims at developing in partners an awareness of their central, disruptive, maladaptive interlocking system of interaction with a view to changing this pattern so that they experience the possibility of an alternative rewarding relationship dynamic. Since this non-productive pattern operates largely on the unconscious level, partners may be aware that something repeatedly 'goes wrong in our communication', but may not understand the nature of the defences operating, nor have an appreciation of the underlying needs that are not being clearly articulated between them. A process that once served a protective function in the family of origin may now be a fixed and rigid pattern of response in certain situations that inhibits intimacy and the open sharing of priorities, needs and feelings.

The principal goal of the brief-term work will be to help partners develop a wider range of response options so that they can interact more effectively and satisfactorily in all areas of their relationship. Being 'stuck' in old patterns of interaction is a common human experience since we all bring to our new relationships the cumulative learning from the past. Some of this learning will have proved helpful, maybe even life-saving, in the original context but may now not serve us so well particularly if the learnt pattern involves suppressing our own needs and feelings or a decision to survive in a state of independent self-sufficiency that does not allow for easy communication of vulnerability with others around us. Relationships involve sharing, mutuality and joint problem-solving capacities. A new relationship will inevitably challenge our old survival patterns, no matter how adaptive these may have been in our families of origin. When two people set up home together, there are two separate and distinct 'family cultures' coming together under one roof. Partners may believe that 'the way we did it in our family was the best way' or perhaps even 'the only way', so that a process of understanding difference will be important in coming to terms with a variety of approaches to the same situation, all of which can have effective results.

In the course of the intervention, the therapist will assist the couple in mobilising their resources and in drawing on the strengths in their relationship which may have become overshadowed by their presenting problems. The desired outcome of brief-term work is for the couple to develop more effective ways of problem-solving and interacting. On this basis they can then decide how they wish to proceed with their relationship. Moving forward in this way presupposes that sufficient promise and good will remains in the relationship to build upon subsequently. There is the possibility in this model of a further six to eight sessions in six to twelve months' time in order to extend and deepen the contact between partners and to deal with any particular 'sticking points' that may be persistent over time and require further intervention from an expert.

Reasonable goals for this type of therapy are necessarily focused and circumscribed by time constraints. We see these therapeutic goals as follows:

1. to facilitate an awareness of the central non-problem solving, repetitive sequence of interaction in the relationship;
2. to disrupt this pattern within the sessions to give partners the opportunity to experience new behaviour that leads to positive/ different outcomes;
3. to assist couples in developing effective problem-solving strategies that lead to conflict resolution;
4. to outline and mobilise the strengths in the relationship;
5. to pinpoint strategies to remedy deficits where realistic and possible.

The attainment of these goals will inevitably be influenced by certain factors that relate to motivation, to the couple's particular relationship history and to individual needs and life stages. A primary factor in achieving a successful outcome in our experience is the good will of the two people involved in the partnership. We sometimes refer to this as 'having energy for the relationship'. This relates to a willingness to put in effort to achieve desired changes and the sense that remaining in the relationship is worth while. Such a willingness to accept that change is both necessary and important is a basic starting point for any effective work. The first sessions may well involve an investigation of the attitudes of the partners towards one another and an honest assessment of where their loyalties and energies lie. Straight talking about feelings, dealing with resentments from the past and recognising differences in values may be a prerequisite for a contract to work on improving the relationship. The prognosis for effective change is in our experience more highly related to the willingness of people to engage with the problem than on the severity of the situation between them. For this reason it is very important for the therapist not to prejudge a situation on minimal initial information, for instance from a referral source, but to set aside assumptions and prejudices in an open effort to be present for the two people who have come for help.

A challenge for the therapist arises when the partners do not agree upon the definition of the problem area. Although this will be focused on a particular content arena in the relationship, it primarily reflects a process problem related to very different frames of reference and ways of construing reality. For example, if one partner believes that there is a problem in a certain area and the other either denies the existence of the problem or sees it as an insignificant aspect of the relationship, no effective problem-solving is possible until there is agreement about (a) what the problem is and (b) its importance to both partners. 'I think our main problem is that we seldom talk about our feelings for one another any more' responded to by 'I think that is an exaggeration. Any way, given the busy lives we lead with jobs, children and friends, I don't know where I am supposed to find the time to whisper sweet nothings in your ear!' Such a disagreement about what matters in the relationship is probably what has brought the couple for therapy and the significance for each person of the feelings, needs and beliefs underlying their statements will be the therapist's first concern. The partners in this example appear to be at odds about the importance that sharing feelings should assume in their relationship. It is not for the therapist to impose a point of view upon them; rather to explore the importance to each of them of their particular view of this facet of relationship. It may well turn out that they come from families or cultures that varied greatly in the expression of feelings so that the partners are reflecting what for each of them has constituted their reality up to this time. An understanding of this difference is critical to change on both sides.

If an agreement about the definition of the problem is not present at the outset, then the focus of the brief-term intervention may well be to investigate this discrepancy and its meaning for the relationship. Such an investigation may reveal underlying differences of need, expectations, priorities and frames of reference in the partners. Sometimes this therapeutic process leads to a basic and far-reaching re-negotiation of the parameters of the relationship to take cognizance of the differing needs of each partner. In one particular instance Mahmoud wished to pursue a career in business and remain in the context of his extended family whilst Rashida had always held the image of a peaceful life in a rural setting reminiscent of her childhood in Kenya where she could develop her pottery business with the luxury of the countryside within easy access. Whereas on the face of it these needs appeared incompatible, through understanding and negotiation around these divergent priorities, they were able to agree a resolution that involved a move to a rural setting within easy commuting distance of the city. Both of them had previously imagined that the other was incapable of either understanding the importance of the needs involved or willing to tolerate the differences. Although the final solution seems an obvious compromise, the issue dealt with in therapy was the process of problem resolution which was reflected in the current critical example. Couples involved in struggles of this kind have often become polarized in their demands. They may have reached a point where they have begun to believe that their frames of reference are irreconcilable. This may finally turn out to be the case, but in many of the examples from our practice, when people are given the space to express their views in a safe and contained atmosphere, they realize that they have misunderstood and 'missed' one another in their anxiety that they themselves will not be heard and understood in turn.

In dealing with problem definition in the therapy sessions, we have found the work of Schiff *et al.* (1975) relating to the concept of 'discounting' extremely useful. They define discounting as 'an internal mechanism which involves people minimizing or ignoring some aspect of themselves, others, or the reality situation,' Schiff *et al.* (1975,

(p. 14). In the simplest sense, a person may ignore their own needs or the needs of the other person or simply deny some aspect of the situation. Such a process of discounting will mean that a person is assessing a situation without taking crucial factors into account. Schiff and her colleagues have classified different types, areas and levels of discounting. For example, a partner can discount the existence of a problem stated by the other: 'I don't know what she is going on about; I think our sex life is normal for people who have been married as long as we have. Why, what does she expect after all these years . . .'; or the significance of a problem: 'Of course, we do sometimes have a problem getting together to talk, but it is by no means as serious as he suggests. Then he has always been given to exaggeration!'; or one partner can discount the possibility of change in a particular area: 'Sure we don't often share deeply and I sometimes miss that in our relationship; but then I don't believe that human beings have the capacity to sustain long-term intimate relationships. Ours is as good as it gets, so why tilt at windmills!'; or one partner can discount his own ability to change a particular aspect of a situation: 'Sure I know she has a point in wanting me to share my feelings as her friends do; the problem is I never have been nor ever will be the sort of feely-feely person she longs for!'

Unless partners can agree on the definition of a problem, on its importance (severity) in their relationship and on their own capacity to make changes with regard to the issue under discussion, there is little space for manoeuvre. The examples we have given above range from the more severe to the less severe in terms of levels of discounting. It is often much more of a challenge to deal with someone who does not acknowledge that there is a problem at all, than with someone who is struggling only with their own capacity to change in a certain area. A large part of the challenge for the brief-term therapist will be to arrive at a common definition and agreement about the area which will serve as the focus for change. If two people are discounting at different levels both of them will experience being misunderstood and they will probably argue fiercely to uphold their own definition of 'reality'.

In agreeing a contract in brief-term work it is crucial therefore that the partners agree on the definition and severity of the problem, otherwise much of the discussion will be undermined by this basic difference in frames of reference. Such a struggle to agree about what is a significant issue in a relationship may reveal deep-seated discrepancies in world views related to differences in values and priorities in life. For example, a couple may discover that the importance that one person places on career success may not be shared by the other, who would much prefer a less hurried, scaled down life materially, that offers more time for closeness and family interaction. Such very basic choices about life style may underpin the many problematic interactions that characterize the relationship. Unless this discrepancy is clarified, any work on improving communication skills may fall on infertile ground.

Characteristically couples present with somewhat differing problems at different stages of their relationship. In the early years, people often bring to therapy the issue of coming to terms with the discovery of difference between them – the realization that they are two very different people with their own values and assumptions! This may for example involve the question about whether they wish to get married at all since this may be important to one partner and not to the other, who may regard marriage as socially or legally unattractive or unnecessary. Another issue that we are now meeting more frequently in our therapy with couples is the question of whether people wish to share one home or continue to live separately in their own homes, even after marriage. Sometimes this may involve living in different parts of the country due to job demands. Partners at this beginning stage may also be dealing with the impact of a first child on their closeness. Sexual problems are also often a focus at this juncture as people begin to uncover differences in pace, rhythm, experience and need. Generally the aim of a brief-term intervention in these early years could be summarized as: 'We can disagree and still co-operate!' Learning to negotiate differences and developing conflict resolution skills is vital at this stage. Especially in cases where partners have assumed a strong agreement about crucial issues that turns out to be ill-founded, the disillusionment that arises from coming up sharply against the reality of different frames of reference may prove an insuperable challenge to the parties concerned. 'If you really loved me the way you said you did, you could never consider taking me away from my family to a strange country . . .'. However, we have found that even in such cases, if good will is present, then the possibility of effective change remains.

In the middle phase, couples often come with child-rearing issues; problems of alienation and distance from one another; and differences in priorities related to time, money, career and friends. Having dealt with the challenges of getting on their feet financially and establishing a family, a couple frequently find that they have grown apart or that early in-built differences between them are having an alienating effect. The fact that both may be very busy with their own careers, interests and responsibilities may for a time disguise the problem until it is highlighted by some external pressure, e.g. one partner establishes a relationship outside the marriage; or a partner becomes ill; a parent dies; or a partner loses a job. The goal of brief-term therapy at this stage is, therefore, frequently the re-establishment of intimacy within a framework that acknowledges and respects individual difference, although some couples may use the sessions to make a decision to go their separate ways.

Remarriage is not uncommon in this middle phase. In the case of second or subsequent marriages, there is the challenge of integrating two families with different values, needs and conventions. In such cases the priorities of one partner concerning children from a previous marriage can give rise to competitiveness, jealousy and insecurity on the part of the other. In an interesting chapter entitled 'Therapy with Remarried Couples' Patricia Papernow (in Wheeler and Backman, 1994) draws attention to some of the particular problems faced by step-families. She points out that frozen insider and outsider positions that may well be viewed as pathological in first-time families may be the normal consequence of the situation in a step-family where parent–child relationships precede the couple's relationship. Assumptions that govern relationships in a first-time family may not appertain here, and the couples therapist is well advised to facilitate the remarried couple to work out their own unique solution to this challenging and ever more frequent occurrence in our contemporary society. It is important to remember, as Papernow also stresses, that children in such situations are often facing multiple losses – of schools, friends and neighbourhood – and may not be coming to the new family with the same undisguised enthusiasm that their parents may be bringing. Isabel Fredericson and Joseph H. Handlon (also in Wheeler and Backman, 1994) further elaborate on some of the problems faced by remarried couples. For example, the present marriage is almost invariably perceived within the context of the previous marriage and contrasted with it, favourably or unfavourably. The blending of two families that have evolved two separate life-styles will require active negotiation for a new blend to work. But as they point out too, remarried partners often expect to work on the relationship and do not automatically assume that all will be well without active effort on their part. This factor may bring them for couples therapy earlier in the life of the relationship than if this were a first-time marriage.

In the later years, differences in energy levels and needs may affect the balance of a relationship and change the power balance between two people. At this stage, there is often the need to consolidate life tasks to achieve a state of 'ego integrity' (Erikson, 1950, p. 259) which may involve a re-evaluation and renewed integration in a core relationship. Once children have left home or the issue of retirement arises, the couple frequently faces anew issues of intimacy, closeness and the challenge of restructuring time. This may involve facing the barrenness and isolation that has set in over years, or consolidating the richness of a relationship that has retained its vitality but where renewed goal setting is required. At this stage couples will also be coming to terms with the reality of the choices that they made earlier in their lives and with what *is* and what *will not be* part of their relationship experience. For some couples, therapy offers an opportunity to open up new channels of communication and new options for enjoying pursuits together without their previous responsibilities. How to deal with the effects of ageing, the impact of illness in one or both partners, differences in sexual energy or needs and adjustment to a slowed-down life-style are issues that are prominent at this time.

The social and cultural context in which the relationship occurs will be of special interest to the therapist, since there may be a clash of frames of reference leading to contradictory expectations of roles in the relationship and expectations of marriage. The woman's role in marriage may be defined in such a way by the culture that this does not leave her free to develop her own career or invest in her own interests. In some cultures there is a pressure on getting married young which later leaves people feeling that they 'have lost out on their youth'. In cross-cultural and inter-racial marriages, there is frequently an issue around the question 'can you really understand me?' In same-sex partnerships, there may be issues about role definitions in the relationship and/or about bearing/adopting/rearing children. Further complexities may ensue from life-stage differences between partners, for example a woman may want children when the man feels 'too young' to cope with that responsibility; or one partner may wish to settle down while the other first wants 'to travel the world'. One partner may already have growing children whereas the other partner may wish for children in this new relationship. Class or caste differences may also place stress on the relationship, where one partner may be implicitly or explicitly defined as inferior by birth to the other. Socio-economic disadvantages may impact powerfully on a couple's interaction. Chronic shortage of resources and the fight to survive may absorb all available energy and leave little time free for intimate exchange.

A couple's particular relationship history may be fraught with memories of constant battles, or have involved multiple losses or be so laden with pain and hurt about previous betrayals that these issues may powerfully colour their every interaction. Whatever the nature of the prior relationship history, this will inevitably take its space in the therapy. A couple may, for instance, have experienced a trauma that has been insufficiently talked about and not resolved between them so that its shadow has fallen over all their subsequent interactions and created an emotional strain that affects their daily lives. Brief therapy can provide a space for the trauma to be addressed and the painful feelings to surface, so that the partners can move forward in their relationship. Regrettably frequent too, is the case where one partner may have been sexually abused as a child or adolescent, and this problem has now surfaced in the couple's relationship and impinges on their sexual and emotional contact. The therapist will often in such instances intervene to help the couple deal with this intrusion from the past in as much as it affects the dynamics of their relationship in the present. More in-depth personal work in individual therapy can effectively support this endeavour.

Other partnerships may have been marked by constant fighting laced with hurtful remarks or by regular rejection of each other characterized by long periods of deliberate silence and withdrawal. An accumulated history of such destructive interactions may seriously interfere with any attempts on either part at direct and open communication. The therapist's task will involve supporting the couple to investigate openly and directly such undermining aspects of their history in the safety of the therapeutic context. 'Held feelings' will be shared in order to create the emotional space for moving forward in a new way. Sometimes, however, people find it impossible to deal with and set aside their history and embark upon a new era in their relationship without constantly referring back to the past. Such a difficulty in 'letting go of the past' may stand in the way of future relating. If people have a greater investment in revenge and proving that 'I am right' than in committing themselves to a process of understanding and negotiating new parameters for the relationship, the couples therapist may not be in the position to intervene effectively in the process between them. We have, however, worked to good effect with partners who experience remorse about the pain that they have inflicted on one another, and are prepared to make reparation for this and wish to repair the damage in their joint lives. A person in individual therapy once reported that her partner who had been inveterately set against any semblance of couples work in an alienated marriage, said to her: 'Your willingness to apologize and accept your part in hurting me has convinced me that all that therapy is not nonsense after all . . . I feel ready to attend some couples sessions if we both do that and stop blaming each other.' Happy events do not only belong in fairy tales, but the hard work involved in the reconstruction of this relationship took dedicated effort on the part of therapist and clients alike!

Whatever the particular issues involved, the task for the brief-term therapist is to focus on the central process dynamic that is hindering the couple from discussing their issues in a clear and straight manner to reach a problem resolution. It is our contention that the primary work needs to be at a process resolution level; however, we will of course deal with particular matters in the sessions as examples of 'raw material' to be tackled with alternative, problem-solving strategies. In our experience whatever the immediate focus for the couple (which may change from session to session, and in their perception is the cause of the conflict) the underlying process tends to repeat itself. Rachel and Simon start off arguing about money and then very quickly bring in their conflicts about parents-in-law. In both instances the process is one where Simon blames Rachel for her insensitivity and lack of foresight whilst she bursts into tears feeling misunderstood and then withdraws from him and refuses further discussion.

One of the central process issues that is invariably addressed is the need for specificity and clearly defined contracts and agreements between people. In this sense the distinction between content and process becomes artificial, since at that level the content of the session is the process of contract-making. What Rachel and Simon finally agreed involved Simon making specific requests of Rachel without blame or generalization, while she agreed to respond directly to his request and not avoid contact by withdrawing 'hurt and devastated'. This specific behavioural contract helped them to break through the current impasse in their relationship and provided them with an alternative method of dealing with problem areas. The brief-term therapist may well start by focusing the couple in a specific behavioural way in order to open up the route to more complex emotional interaction that has become lost in the constant stand-offs between partners. A task that can be clearly defined and described will seem manageable in times of difficulty and instil hope of change in an otherwise bleak situation. Small changes can then lead to more significant reversals of destructive patterns of interaction that are undermining the fabric of the relationship.

In the process of assessment and history-taking, the therapist will gain a sense of the strengths in the relationship and a knowledge of what contribution each partner makes to support or undermine the process between them. An important consideration will be how resilient each partner is in response to straight talk and direct feedback from the other. In our assessment of the partners' strengths, we may also enquire how they have previously dealt with problems similar to the one they are presenting, perhaps in another related context. One person reported how in a work environment he was very effectively able to state his own opinions clearly, whereas in his relationship with his wife he tended to get confused and be confusing so that she ended up getting irritated with him and ignoring his requests. With some assistance in the therapy session, he was able to mobilize his resources and implement in his intimate relationship the same skills that he could so effectively apply in the less emotionally laden atmosphere at his workplace. A focus on the people's existing skills and problem-solving abilities is empowering for them. The therapist's task will be to facilitate this transfer of learning from one situation to another and in this process uncover the emotional blocks that have prevented someone from doing this spontaneously.

We take from the gestalt approach the concepts of 'self support' and 'environmental support' (Delisle, 1988) to assess a person's capacity for handling stress and challenge effectively. Self-support refers to the manner in which people are able to contain anxiety and use their thinking, feeling and behaviour to enhance their understanding of self and others. People's use of environmental support refers to their capacity to relate to the physical world effectively and to draw comfort and support from the significant others in their personal world. In order to solve problems effectively, people use a combination of self-support and environmental support. Our own particular histories may have biased us to deny ourselves support of either kind even though this may be readily available to us or may have slanted us to depend too heavily on ourselves or too heavily on others in our daily lives and in our relationship styles.

In assessing the level of self-support and environmental support a person is able to sustain, the therapist will gain an image of the relative strengths that people bring to a partnership. For example, some people will impulsively blurt out whatever is on their mind without assessing the impact of their utterings on others, and then be shocked and perhaps even incapacitated by an angry response. Such a person may not have assessed the situation correctly and may lack the awareness of the effect of their behaviour on another. It is reasonable to expect that if you say something derogatory to another (e.g. 'You are a wimp and I'm sorry I ever got involved with you') the other person is likely to be angry and hurt by the comment. A lack of such elementary knowledge of the nature of interaction betokens a basic lack of cognitive self-support and insight into interpersonal relationships. It is not difficult to see that such a process may alienate people in the environment, leaving the person concerned isolated and unsupported. The brief-term therapist will have the task of educating such people in effective and straight ways of expressing anger (e.g. I get angry when you complain about me in the company of our friends. Please tell me privately what upsets you . . .). Another person may be chronically indecisive and deliberate endlessly before taking action. In a close relationship such a person may not get to the point of stating their own position or responding in an appropriate manner to the other, stuck instead in frozen inactivity. The focus in therapy will be on the acquisition of skills that enable people to increase awareness of their needs and feelings and to communicate these in ways that are likely to lead to mutual understanding and need fulfilment. Such understanding is a prerequisite for effective negotiation.

The scope and boundaries of brief therapy with couples in a six-to-eight session intervention may be summarized as follows:

1. to identify central process problems;
2. to increase awareness of the interlocking, non-problem-solving nature of repetitive processes or 'games' (Berne, 1961);
3. to facilitate partners to try out some new behaviours to realize how change can be effected;
4. to pinpoint strengths and deficits in the relationship and assist people in mobilizing existing resources in new situations;
5. to help develop new strategies to remedy deficit where possible;
6. to instil the hope that change is possible, yet to foster the idea that change needs to be balanced with acceptance.

2

STRENGTHS AND LIMITATIONS OF BRIEF THERAPY WITH COUPLES

STRENGTHS

(a) The strength of brief therapy with couples lies principally in the short, sharp focused work aimed at very specific goals which can open the relationship up sufficiently for people to proceed in that vein. Often such a focused intervention is sufficient to interrupt a destructive or undermining dynamic in the relationship and once again put people in touch with their own capacity for nurturing and creative relating. In our experience any couple may reach a crisis point, often related to internal changes in one or both partners or to external life-related events impinging on the couple that catapult people into outdated, non-problem-solving feelings, thoughts and behaviours. An appropriately placed and directed series of interventions into this unhelpful, often archaic interlocking process is frequently sufficient for couples again to touch into their love for one another and explore other co-operative solutions to problems. The therapist can assist them in mobilizing their inner resources and drawing on what has previously worked well between them. Brief-term therapy also offers people the opportunity of learning new problem-solving strategies in the contained environment provided by psychotherapy. There are also other related advantages to brief therapy with couples.

(b) Brief-term therapy with a couple minimizes the chances of the therapist's triangulation into the relationship dynamics. It leaves the therapist free to make the appropriate interventions into the system and then to withdraw so that the protagonists are once again facing one another without the presence of a third person in the process. In longer-term work with couples we believe that the therapist runs the risk of becoming part of the system in some essential way, so that the people 'need' the therapist's presence for adjudication or protection purposes and have difficulty in solving problems on their own. In such instances it is not unusual for one partner to say: 'I kept this for our session here because I was too scared to mention it at home' or 'I knew you would take me seriously and listen to me if I brought this here . . .'. This may then mean that the therapist has become central to the problem-solving and negotiation process. The aim of any intervention in couples work is to facilitate development by the partners of their own understanding of the dynamic of their relationship and develop their skills in dealing with this creatively, independently of the therapist.

This presents a challenge for the therapist since it is vital for the success of brief-term work that she make the maximum impact on the relationship in the time frame available, and at the same time does not in any way 'take over' the problem-solving process from the clients and leave them feeling de-skilled and inadequate. This is not to imply, however, that some initial dependence on the therapist is not both important and necessary – after all, it is for the therapist's input that people seek help in the first instance! The therapist may be regarded as an expert, objective observer of the process between two people, and one who has no direct personal investment in the relationship beyond that of doing his professional job. Brief-term therapy offers the couple an opportunity to receive reflections on their interactive process from a trained observer of human nature in order to help them resolve a relational impasse. From the point of view of the therapist, the interventions will be concise, to the point and facilitative of the process. The therapist needs to be alert to any countertransference reactions that may interfere with his ability to remain in a professional role to the couple. In this regard we have found particularly helpful the concept of the 'drama triangle' (Karpman, 1968) which outlines the stances people take when their unconscious processes begin to interfere with their avowed, conscious intentions in an interaction. By reflecting on the signs that a person may be 'rescuing' (sentimentality or smugness at being clever) or 'persecuting' (wanting to press home a point to show you are right or the tendency to say 'I told you so') or 'feeling victimised' (feeling taken advantage of), the therapist can identify common countertransferential traps and avoid these. Although being triangulated into the couple's process in these ways is possible in brief-term therapy, the time-limited nature and sharp focus of this work makes it less likely that the therapist will become unhealthily involved in the couple's process. The contractual basis in the approach we outline in this book also acts as a protection for all parties concerned since this helps to keep the work 'on track'.

(c) The sense of being evaluated and 'judged' by an observer is always a risk in couple's work, since the therapist is constantly negotiating a delicate balance between support and confrontation and can easily be experienced by one partner as favouring the other's perspective over their own. Because the therapist is engaged with a couple for a limited number of sessions, it is often easier to maintain a neutral role, without bias towards one person or the other in the relationship. Longer-term therapy is well known to encourage and foster the transference onto the therapist, which then needs to be worked through in the sessions. Brief-term therapy with its main focus on the working alliance (Greenspan, 1965) between therapist and couple minimizes the transference.

However, because two people are involved as clients jointly in the therapy, there is always some possibility that one or the other will feel judged and evaluated by certain of the therapist's comments. This is a particular problem with couples whose central dynamic involves looking for a judge or an adjudicator to 'tell them' who is right and who is wrong in the relationship. This is akin to what was labelled by Berne (1964) the game of 'Courtroom' in which a judge is sought to pronounce sentence; the 'guilty' party ends up branded as the persecutor, and the 'acquitted' party as the triumphant and exonerated 'innocent' victim rescued from taking responsibility for any part of the process, whilst the problem remains unaddressed! The final move in this game often involves the couple turning on the therapist who ends up as the final 'victim' of the process. It is vital for the therapist to state openly that his/her task is not one of judgement. After all, the problem is not about whose frame of reference is 'right' or 'wrong' but to achieve greater mutual understanding of diversity. This position of neutrality is easier to hold in brief-term therapy where the risk of countertransference involvement is controlled by the sharp focus and time constraints of the intervention. Every couple's therapist can probably attest to the seductive pull to 'take sides' and express a judgement from on high. Any such temptation is usually an indicator that the therapist has overlooked or minimized some essential aspect of the encounter between herself and the couple or between the partners themselves. In such a case, it is wise to take stock, check out with the clients what has been understood or overlooked and to re-evaluate the agreed contractual focus.

(d) Brief-term therapy also has the advantage that it exposes the couple's most intimate secrets to a third person for a limited time only. This reduces the possibility of people feeling shamed and 'exposed' to an outsider or a 'watcher' – a greater potential risk in couple's therapy than in individual work. Brief therapy minimizes this inevitable 'voyeuristic' element in couples work. Because as a practitioner you are given a view into very intimate areas of the couple's shared lives together, this inevitably creates a sense of spectatorship for them and for the therapist. People are especially vulnerable to shame in this context, so the brief therapeutic encounter holds the advantage that they are 'in and out' of the 'exposing' situation in a relatively short time and can then consolidate once again the holding boundary around the intimacy of their shared space.

We know from the extensive literature on shame and shame-based systems (Kaufman, 1993; Nathanson, 1992) that the experience of shame learnt in the family of origin can easily be replicated in a therapeutic setting. If people have been repeatedly shamed when feeling certain emotions or expressing their basic human needs, they will tend to develop a 'shame-bind' linked to a particular emotion or experience (Kaufman, 1993). Some examples follow: 'I feel so ashamed to be exposed and seen when I am upset like this'; 'I feel ashamed . . . humiliated . . . when you point out that I don't share my scare . . .'; 'I can't get past the feeling that sex is something nasty . . . to be ashamed of . . . even though my head tells me otherwise . . . it's so degrading to be human . . . .' If the therapist pushes for or insists on the expression of an affect or a need linked to such a shame-bind then the particular partner in focus will experience shame in the therapeutic setting. This process will not promote change, since people tend to withdraw under the impact of shame and hide away those tender parts of themselves that may just have begun to appear in the relationship. Because the couples therapist is an observer of the very intimate areas of people's lives, the possibility of evoking shame is fairly high. In some sense, the risk of shame is even greater than in individual therapy where the person is 'seen' only by one other person, whereas in couples therapy, if the shame of one person is activated, then there will be two onlookers and the sense of 'audience' is there. Because of the focused contractual nature of this model of brief-term therapy, the clients share with the therapist the control of the therapeutic content and negotiate with one another and with the therapist what areas are open for discussion at a particular time. This process tends to minimize the likelihood that shame-binds will suddenly and unexpectedly be activated, which would replicate the original traumatic events. If this does happen it may lead to the premature termination of the therapy and possibly even discourage the couple from seeking further assistance elsewhere. A clear agreement between partners that their exchanges will not involve shaming one another, blaming the other or using abusive language or name-calling will do much to prevent shame-binds from being reactivated by the therapy.

(e) Any previous experience that the people involved have had of seeking assistance or relying on authority figures will profoundly affect the nature of their expectations of the therapist and the use of the therapeutic space. It will, therefore, be of great help to the brief-term therapist to enquire at the outset about the individual's expectations, fears and hopes of the therapy so that these issues can be immediately and realistically addressed. It will also be of assistance to check how each member of the couple views the therapist's role in the process. For example, 'I think that you will be the referee . . .' requires some immediate careful discussion and clarification! In this regard, it is important to consider the issue of power in the therapeutic relationship. It is inevitable that the therapist will be vested with power by the clients, some of this deriving from his professional status and expertise, and some related to his perceived power as an authority who can pronounce what is 'right or wrong' about relationships. French and Raven's work of 1960, quoted in E. Holloway (1995), defines legitimate power as 'a person's perceived trustworthiness as a professional, socially sanctioned provider of services' and expert power as that 'attributed to a person because of his or her mastery of knowledge and skills'. Clients will seek out therapists because they perceive them as possessing power of these kinds and for this reason request their assistance. It is an ongoing challenge to exercise this power in a way that consistently benefits the client and does not serve the needs of the therapist. An advantage in brief-term work is that the contact will be short and will be focused on jointly negotiated goals, so that there is immediately more of a shared power base than in approaches where goals are not openly negotiated and agreed. The time limit also ensures that longer-term issues of dependency and seeking need gratification from the therapist are not as likely to be evoked. The fact that the focus is on maintaining a working alliance underpinned by contracting also discourages regressive behaviour which could not be effectively dealt with in this type of brief encounter. In a climate in which the abuse of therapist power is under constant scrutiny, brief-term therapy has the advantage of not fostering long-term dependency in clients (or therapists) and of focusing on mutually agreed targets, so that the therapist's own agenda is carefully monitored by the very process that underpins the philosophical basis of the intervention. It is crucial in this regard for the therapist to address in supervision his/her own counter-transference feelings so that the information elicited and the interventions made are geared to the health of the couple and do not begin to reflect the therapist's own needs or interests in the situation. The specific focus of brief therapy makes this ascetic discipline both easier and more possible to maintain. Where skilfully applied, it is an economic and elegant form of therapeutic enterprise.

LIMITATIONS

(a) Brief-term therapy does not allow for the consolidation of new patterns of behaviour in the course of therapy. The therapist's efforts are confined to interrupting repetitive and outmoded patterns of interaction; she does not have the time nor the opportunity to support and assist the couple in maintaining new styles of interaction. A brief-term intervention allows for the demonstration and experience of alternative behaviour between people, but they need to have both the ego strength and the powers of self-observation to use this new-found learning after the end of the therapeutic intervention. The aim is for the couple to experience using alternative strategies and problem-solving behaviours in the sessions and as 'homework' in between so that they know and have felt the effects of these new options for interaction. Although the time period does, therefore, allow for some repetition and confirmation of new skills, it does not provide for the consolidation of this relearning over time with the availability of an expert's help when the process goes wrong. This more prolonged contact with an expert may be essential for some people. There can be no doubt that in some cases, the partners will require the help of a therapist over time especially where there has been a significant deficit in socialization in their early years and there has not been the opportunity to remedy this in adulthood. Therapy then becomes a longer-term re-education process where the therapist is working primarily to remedy the deficit in very basic communication skills and strategies for conflict management. Such severe deficit is usually the result of repetitive trauma in childhood that has interfered significantly with the development of normal relationship experiences.

(b) The main limitation of brief therapy with couples is that it simply may not reach deep-seated personal issues that are confounding the relationship. This is particularly true where basic trust in others has been affected by traumatic childhood abuse and neglect, whether this be psychological or physical or both. In these cases a longer-term couples therapy, supported by individual therapy for the partners, may be the more appropriate choice.

By the very nature of the process, the effectiveness of a brief intervention will be determined by the accuracy with which the central process dynamic can be addressed. However, even if this is identified, there may be long-standing resentments and hurts that prevent a movement forward or deep-seated personal conflicts may lead to an inability on one or both parts to mobilize the resources to deal constructively with the issues in focus. Should this be the case, a different type of therapy may be recommended. This type of situation will usually reveal itself at the assessment interview.

However, even where the central destructive dynamic is identified and successfully challenged in the brief therapy, the deeper levels of the conflict uncovered in this process may only be touched upon in the context of the aims of the brief work. Our position is substantially in agreement with that of Solomon, who writes:

> Couples who have relationship problems, but do not have a history of severe narcissistic injury, may resolve differences through compromise, problem-solving, improved communication or through acknowledgement, acceptance and negotiation of some basic differences . . . . When there is a history of narcissistic vulnerability and failure of the other to provide necessary emotional supplies, the result is that small arguments may cause an experience of fragmentation and emotional destruction – a loss of ability to think clearly and a reaction of either rage or total withdrawal. (Solomon, 1992, p. 47)

(c) The need for the rapid establishment of an effective working alliance in brief therapy requires that sufficient trust in the therapist and the process of therapy be built up within the initial session for the work to start immediately. This will, in turn, depend upon the willingness of the couple to be open about their process with a stranger. Trust in the therapist's ability to be of assistance is a crucial element. If, for instance, one or both of the partners is chronically suspicious and mistrustful, then the establishment of a working alliance may not be possible within the time available. People who can be helped in brief-term work exhibit the capacity to make an adult-to-adult contract about their needs and goals, display sufficient ego strength to accept and deal with confrontation and possess the ability and willingness to reflect on their own process. If these qualities are not present, it is unlikely that brief therapy will help, and a different form of treatment will be recommended. This requirement places a limitation on the couples who can be assisted in a six-to-eight session intervention. We are clear that it is important not to make exaggerated claims for work of this kind and to use it only where it is likely to be beneficial, ethical and meet the current needs of the couple. However, we do not under-estimate the aspect of personal motivation which remains one of the most significant elements contributing to the success of our work with couples and will sometimes override all the qualifications we have made to the choice of this kind of work.

(d) In addition, since the goal of brief therapy is to focus on and address the central disabling dynamic in the relationship, the therapist will not be able to monitor the relationship much beyond the scope of this intervention. It will, of course, be possible to name other problem areas and point to avenues for exploration, but their investigation will not form part of the contract in the brief work. We are making the assumption that most relationships tend to founder and get stuck around a central process issue, and that if we can tackle this in the brief therapy we may be able to free the partners enough to proceed productively. We appreciate that such a result may be modest in comparison to what may be desired (especially by the therapist who may be aware of complexities in the relationship that the clients could productively address). However, we are the first to acknowledge that breaking through the central relationship impasse is not always possible within this frame, and that in certain relationships the problems are manifold and wide-reaching so that long-term therapy may hold the only hope of resolution. We will take this issue up again in discussing the assessment of the relationship dimensions.

Finally all work with couples will require consideration of what can and what cannot be changed in a particular relationship. For example if one partner demands that the other change from being a quiet introvert into a gregarious extrovert, the first person will need to modify his/her expectations regarding change in accordance with what is likely given basic temperamental variables. In another case, a partner may be prepared to make only certain changes and not others, even where these are possible, because of different priorities or core beliefs. For example, if one partner wishes to become a missionary and work in the Third World, the other may not be prepared to make such an accommodation; or, one partner may desire a monogamous relationship, whilst the other does not wish to relinquish the option of having other sexual contacts. The discussion may then devolve around the issues that are negotiable and those that are non-negotiable in the relationship. The therapist's task will be to enable the partners to state their position clearly and unambiguously so that the other is not left in doubt about what is likely or possible. In this sense, the therapist's office frequently provides a safe context in which people put into words the previously 'unsaid and unsayable'. Once the parameters for future discussion have been laid in a frank and unambiguous manner, further negotiations between partners can then take place. An open and honest look at the reality of the relationship will often lead to a creative re-evaluation of what each partner may reasonably hope to gain from it.

Challenging the illusions and unrealistic expectations that have been secretly held by partners is perhaps the least enviable task a couples therapist faces. In this regard it is vital for the therapist to monitor carefully the nature of their own assumptions and illusory hopes, lest they enter into a collusion with the clients which prevents the attainment of the style of intimacy that is possible between these two people. We are supported in this task of bringing into awareness the illusions that people invariably carry (amply supported by media images) by our belief that honesty, openness and a clear view of the realities of the relationship provide the best prognosis for future work. Above all, the challenge for the therapist is to strike the balance between confrontation and acceptance, in a non-judgmental framework. The challenge for the couple is to work for change, while at the same time learning and accepting where this is not likely or possible!

3

AN INTEGRATIVE
THEORETICAL MODEL
FOR BRIEF THERAPY
WITH COUPLES

We have chosen to call our approach to couples therapy an integrative model because it draws on concepts from humanistic, cognitive–behavioural and psychoanalytic sources. This model involves focusing on unhelpful, sometimes even destructive, frames of reference and irrational belief systems that reinforce one another, resulting in a negative interlocking system in which people find themselves trapped within the relationship. Although our primary focus is on identifying the negative interlock or central game that sabotages the communication between two people, our aim in identifying this unhelpful process is to help people find alternative and more creative ways of communication. Such a rigid interlocking pattern can undermine the relationship between partners, especially if the negative reinforcement continues over years and years of futile unsatisfactory interaction. People often show a tendency to get stuck in one form of relating that becomes habitual to them even though they have at their disposal other options that may have worked successfully for them in the past. Their access to these in their current situation may be blocked by resentments linked with accumulated hurts. On occasion they are blocked by the fear that if they show one another any further vulnerability, this will be manipulated to their disadvantage. This is essentially a protective manoeuvre and can be identified as such in the safety of the therapeutic setting.

THE CORE INTERPERSONAL SCHEMA

object
relation

In identifying the central pattern in each partner's process, we have found extremely useful the concept of the 'core interpersonal schema' (Beitman, 1992, p. 207) which includes the beliefs that each person has about self and others and the nature of relationship. 'The basic elements of the core interpersonal schema are two figures in relationship to each other. Usually one of the two figures is dominant and the other is submissive.' (Beitman, 1992, p. 207). The dominance–submission polarity is fairly common as Beitman points out, but there are, of course, many other polarities that derive from people's individual histories. Another frequent polarity in couples therapy is the issue of merging with the other versus independent or solitary action. Finding a balance between such polarized concepts of relating constitutes one of the central challenges of brief-term therapy. The core interpersonal schema comprises our own unique view of ourselves as people (our self-concept) and our expectations of others. From each of our own individual background experience of core relationships we derive certain beliefs about the nature of human interaction which, for better or for worse, influence our expectations of future relationships. In this sense we carry within us a record of all our relationship experiences, dating back to our primary caretakers which remain part of the internal map that governs and influences our subsequent interactions with people. In this context we have found the contribution of object relations theory and its humanistic developments, transactional analysis and gestalt psychotherapy, and of self-psychology extremely relevant. We have also found Anthony Ryle's discussion of 'reciprocal role procedures' (Ryle, 1992, p. 97) in cognitive–analytic therapy an accessible and related theory.

It is somewhat daunting to realize that each of us carries within us a detailed relationship record, albeit much of it outside of conscious awareness, which may subtly or grossly affect our subsequent partnerships. Of course in the process of our experience, we will be both consciously and unconsciously updating our inner maps in response to our current experience. In this sense all of us are involved in an ongoing process of adapting and changing in relation to events in our lives as we make meaning out of these. Some of our experience will challenge our earlier assumptions and lead to changes in our 'core interpersonal schema'; however, other experiences may serve to reinforce and confirm the beliefs we already carry, whether these be very limiting or facilitative of relationship. Negative contacts with people may simply reinforce an already pessimistic view of relationship possibilities based on repeated past disappointments, trauma or abuse ('This just proves once again that it doesn't pay to trust anyone'). Rewarding contacts may either challenge our assumptions ('Perhaps it is possible to be close to someone after all . . .') or support our faith in positive human contact. However, there is also the likelihood that when people do reach out to us, we may redefine this in some negative way to fit in with an existing relationship schema based on a past that has yielded little of a rewarding nature ('She does seem to be open and generous but I need to be careful – she is probably out to use me. People can be so clever in the way they manipulate . . .'). Since much of this process is occurring outside of our conscious awareness, we may be left asking 'Why does this always happen to me?' or 'What have I done wrong this time?' as we face one more failed relationship attempt.

THE CORE INTERPERSONAL SCHEMA SHAPES SUBSEQUENT RELATIONSHIPS

From an intersubjective perspective predicated on internalized object relations, we carry within us a wealth of interpersonal possibilities taken in from our past experiences with significant others by the processes of introjection, identification and imitation. We carry the history not only of our own responses but also the record in memory of the responses of the others we have engaged with significantly, particularly in childhood. This network of interactions forms the basis from which the core interpersonal schema is derived. We have access to our own experience of people and also to our internalized experience of their accumulated reactions to us in related instances. In any interaction we may project onto the other person one of the 'reciprocal roles' (Ryle, 1992) from our internal world, while we move into the corresponding role. In transactional analysis terms, this means that I may move into a Parent ego state while projecting onto my partner the corresponding Child ego state which represents myself as a child of a particular age and stage ('Don't be silly, you are so embarrassing when you get all weepy and weak'). The reverse of course could equally well happen; I may slip into a dependent Child ego state whilst appealing to be taken care of by a 'parent', to whom I ascribe both omnipotence and omniscience ('I just can't help it . . . I have no idea how to sort this out. You seem to have all the know-how!') When I am behaving in this particular way outside of my own conscious awareness, I will not be responding to the other person in terms of current reality, but rather in terms of past encoded patterns from my own relationship history that may be more or less helpful in the present. The more limited, rigid and widely polarized the reciprocal roles in my interpersonal repertoire, the fewer options available to me in any situation. For example, in relation to anger, if I only have available a model of destructive anger offset at the other end of the spectrum by a model for submitting to rage without complaint ('taking it all in') then I am likely to lack anything in the middle of the range, such as options for asserting my own rights and setting limits when others attempt to bully me. Rigid and fixed patterns from the past may severely limit my opportunities for gratifying relationships in the present.

In this context, it is vital to distinguish, however, between vibrant ongoing learning from my experience of relating to others that becomes part of my adaptive repertoire in the world of today, and those unresolved relationship issues from my past that lead to stereotyped non-productive patterns of interaction – the 'games' (Berne,1964) related to my particular relationship script. In the process of growing up and maturing, people will develop flexible, open ways of relating where they are supported to bond with others and learn the process of mutual need satisfaction in a healthy environment. Where support for such learning is freely given and where the contact with significant others is mutually rewarding, people will develop trust in engaging in future relationships. However, even in an optimal environment people are likely to encounter some deficits in their caretakers at home or at school or as the result of environmental trauma, leading to inevitable limiting conclusions about life's possibilities which may unnecessarily hamper them in their subsequent contacts with people.

These limiting conclusions may have been very accurately based on the person's actual experiences in particular specified contexts, but when they are generalised to the world at large and to all people they lose their validity: 'I learnt my lesson well at boarding school – never show any sign of weakness, don't let on that something hurts and that way you'll survive'. Such a conclusion may have served a person well in the context of a tough boarding school, but when applied to intimate relationships will lead to little sharing and consequently limit the opportunity for intimacy and for receiving support in times of need. Such a person may defend against any show of vulnerability by assuming a distant independent stance, leading the other person to withdraw in uncertainty especially if this is reinforced by a complementary experience ('I am not really lovable and others don't want me around – it was always like that at home and with any friends I tried to make at school'). The likely result of such a process is often that the underlying needs of both people get lost in the ensuing misunderstanding. This example illustrates the dynamics of a psychological game (Berne, 1964) which is perpetuated outside of the conscious awareness of both parties and is directly related to those conclusions that make up the essentials of the core interpersonal schema.

To the extent that we have unresolved relationship issues from the past, we may find that we repeat with our current partners such repetitive 'stuck' places. This is the process which Berne (1964) referred to as the 'games people play'. When people are in such a 'game' their behaviour tends to be stereotyped and repetitive and they are given to using familiar phrases that are often repeated at times of conflict: 'you don't understand me . . .'; 'you never listen to anything I say'; 'there we go again, as far as you're concerned it's me, me, me . . .'; 'why don't you admit that you no longer love me . . .'. We each have our familiar recording that tends to come to the fore when we feel trapped and unable to resource ourselves with new options of behaviour, feeling or thinking in particular situations. Such 'stuck places' become the raw material of the couples sessions. As discussed in the previous paragraph, such games are related to protective manoeuvres people decide upon in contexts where their normal human feelings and needs were neither welcomed nor supported by the people around them at the time. Under stress and pressure, people may shut down on feelings, needs and experiences that are unacceptable to others and develop protective patterns that disguise their underlying experience. These patterns may become fixed and rigid over time so that they become recognizable features of the individual's personality style. In that sense people will perpetuate behavioural responses that have served to 'protect' them from hurt in the past, whatever the current perspective of the observer may indicate to the contrary.

However, each new relationship also offers people the opportunity to deal differently with the creative challenge of relationship and in this sense provides us with an opportunity for healing, growth and enrichment. As we are faced with people who do not fulfil our negative fantasies of human life, we may indeed experience within an intimate relationship reparative elements which restore our faith in the possibility of creative human interaction. We base this possibility in our belief that each person has within themselves the capacity for self-realization, for creative human relationship and for changing their lives. Many people have reported the transformational process that has resulted from a close and rewarding relationship in adult life, whether this be with a mentor, a teacher, a friend or a lover. The humanistic belief in human potential, in the capacity for self-actualization (Maslow, 1970) underpins our value system and informs the work we do with couples. As a consequence of this value base, we support the inherent capacity for growth and change in people, believing that in an atmosphere of support they can tap into their own creative resources and healing potential.

From an intersubjective perspective no two situations are ever exactly the same since the field is constantly changing as different factors impact upon us. Although rigid relationship patterns predicated upon our experience to date may form part of what we bring to each new situation, each new experience also has its own unique dimensions which have never before been constellated in a precisely similar manner. This means that there is always a novel element in all experience, we meet the world anew every moment, which despite our learnt patterns paradoxically opens up novel possibilities. This process gives promise of a new resolution to an old problem in response to changed elements in the current field of our experience. Brief therapy can play a significant role in assisting couples at critical points to break out of a fixed pattern with the input of the therapist, who constitutes a new element in their existing field of experience so that they can move on to a new more creative interaction. The therapist with her skills, knowledge and expertise brings to the work with a couple a dimension external to their relationship which has not previously been part of their interpersonal field. This encounter with the therapist can facilitate a change in the nature of their encounter with one another in this changed context which may then be transferred to the fabric of their daily lives.

The challenge for the couples therapist in brief therapy is to identify the central negative interlocking pattern and offer the partners a protected space in which to challenge this process and experiment with alternative, more creative patterns of interaction. It is not within the

scope of a brief therapist to work in-depth with the unresolved internalized object relationships of each partner; the identification of the
pattern is the main focus for the couples therapist. In this process the
couple will gain important knowledge of their own non-problem-
solving process as well as the part played by the other partner. One of
the main foci of couples therapy is to challenge people to use this
knowledge of one another creatively rather than destructively. In saying this we are making two far-reaching assumptions: (a) that when
people come for help they have the goodwill to work towards change
and (b) that human beings have a need and desire to live in creative
communion. We think these assumptions need to be spelt out so that it
can be established whether they are values that the partners share with
the therapist. If there is disagreement at this level then an effective
working alliance may not be established and the work will flounder
from the outset. A shared value base about how knowledge gained in
the therapy process is used to achieve mutually agreed and mutually
enhancing goals for the partners underpins the whole endeavour. It is
not sufficient to assume from people's presence in the therapy room
that they are committed to reconstruction and the respectful use of
new awarenesses. We believe that an explicit overall agreement to the
frame of the therapeutic process requires a shared acknowledgement
that both the partners and the therapist are not out to harm one another deliberately in any way and will immediately discuss any im-
pressions to the contrary and deal with these in a constructive manner.
We hasten to add that we are not suggesting that painful material will
not be addressed in the sessions, rather we are referring to the manner
in which this will be done in keeping with a respect for all parties
concerned in the therapy.

DEVELOPING THE CORE INTERPERSONAL SCHEMA IN CHILDHOOD

Since our central theoretical concept involves the internalization of
early relationships and the effects of our individual relationship 'maps'
on subsequent adult partnerships, we will give a fairly detailed discussion of this process. In his description of human development, Stern
(1985) talks of how the child builds up, through repeated similar experiences, a representation of interactions that have become generalised
(RIG) of a particular constellation of episodes with a primary carer. The
generalized representation is not a specific memory, rather an abstract

distillation of a number of specific memories that share similar components. 'It is a structure about the likely course of events, based on
average experiences. Accordingly, it creates expectations of actions, of
feelings, of sensations, and so on that can either be met or violated'
(Stern, 1985, p. 97). Such RIGs, built up in our interactions with others,
are related to our core experiences of self in relationship and will
influence the beliefs and expectations integrated into our core interpersonal schema. An example of such a RIG would be that 'if I approach
someone close to me for support, this is likely to be forthcoming'. This
will have been derived from an accumulation of achieving satisfactory
outcomes of this type with people in our life.

Some RIGs related to being with people who have significantly influenced the experience of 'self' for us will have a vital influence on our
subsequent relationship history, either in drawing us towards people
or of injecting us with mistrust of intimacy ('I'm loving and lovable' or
'I'm a nuisance and unwelcome here'). Whenever we experience a
particular set of circumstances, we will recall episodes of a specific
type of interaction with a 'self-regulating other', called 'evoked companions' by Stern. 'The evoked companion is an experience of being
with, or in the presence of, a self-regulating other, which may occur in
or out of awareness' (Stern, 1985, p. 112). Stern likens this concept to
Bowlby's concept of 'working models of the mother'. However, he
points out that any 'working model' will be composed of a series of
RIGs which form the smaller building blocks out of which such representations are created by the child in the course of development.
These prototypic images are based on multiple memories of specific
relationships that have evolved and changed over time. We bring our
own unique constellation of 'working models' of intimate people into
any new relationships that we form. These will inevitably have been
shaped by the events of our individual histories, so that no two
people's working models can ever be identical.

In fact, there is a constant process of updating and change in internalized representations as the person encounters new life situations
and individual differences in people. As these experiences of the other
become internalized and integrated by the child, the specific events
may be lost to conscious memory and the person will proceed on the
basis of working models of others that they have developed over the
course of time and experience. It is, of course, the sum total of 'self
in relationship with another' with all the richness and complexity of

multiple interactions that form the stuff of memory and serve as a resource for future relationship. In that sense my memory comprises a rich network of interactions with the related sensations, feelings, thoughts and behaviours that occurred at the time. A person's working models of relationship are usually so deeply embedded in their experience that they may not be all that aware at the conscious level of the assumptions that govern their interactions with others. They may simply accept their own 'models' as true and valid reflections of everyone's shared experience. This process underlies many of the conflicts we have dealt with in brief-term therapy with couples.

If a person was fortunate enough to grow up in an 'average expectable environment' (Winnicott, 1989, p. 195) then she is more likely to develop RIGs that will serve her well in getting her needs met in a relationship.

> For me, a good-enough mother and good-enough parents and a good-enough home do in fact give most babies and small children the experience of not having been significantly let down. In this way average children have the chance to build up a capacity to believe in themselves and the world – they build a structure on the accumulation of introjected reliability. They are blissfully unaware of their good fortune, and find it difficult to understand those of their companions who carry around with them for life experiences of unthinkable anxiety, and a deficit in the department of introjected reliability. (Winnicott, 1989, p. 196)

A basis of 'introjected reliability' is likely to predispose a person to seek out other similar rewarding relationships in their adult life. Where this process has either been absent or the rewarding contacts very erratic, a child is more likely to develop a mistrust or a sense of extreme caution in relation to others.

Taken one step further, it becomes possible to understand that given a sufficiently similar stimulus, I may move into a response set based on my past experience of significant people in my life that may have little or nothing to do with the person currently in front of me – a situation with which a couples therapist will be all too familiar! I may be suspicious of others' motives and constantly experience them as manipulative or exploitative without much substance in the present, no matter how frequently they may display their genuine concern; or at the other extreme I may be very gullible and ready to trust without sufficient knowledge of the other person's behaviour or values, and catapult myself into a relationship prematurely. A frequent challenge for adults who have not been fortunate enough to introject 'reliability' as children is to learn in their adult life how to judge whether someone is trustworthy or not, and to learn to evaluate the feedback they are receiving from the environment.

The introjected others of childhood and adolescence, with their unique attitudes, feelings, behaviours and expressions, will populate our internal world and form the contents of the Parent ego state (Berne, 1961). At times we will reproduce the behaviour, attitudes and feelings of such an introjected other or 'borrowed' self (Weiss, 1950), without being consciously aware of the origins of this process. For example, Clint would give Tamsin a mini-lecture on the virtues of 'saving her pennies' whenever she wished to discuss the purchase of some essential household item, without any reference to the healthy state of their joint finances. In a session, he was able to see that he was mirroring his father's behaviour which, in the midst of a recession when he was unemployed, had immediate relevance to the family's impoverished circumstances. Each Parental introject will be linked in this way to a specific set of experiences in Child ego state (the RIGs described by Stern), except in rare instances where a single traumatic event has become indelibly fixated in memory and exerts a determining influence on subsequent experiences. 'After that terrifying experience, I resolved never again to trust . . .'. Both the contents of our Parent ego states and the contents of our Child ego states constitute the raw material for the 'reciprocal roles' (Ryle, 1992) that form the basis for our adult interactional styles.

RELATIONSHIP ROLES FORM THE BASIS OF A COUPLE'S INTERACTION

In the course of development each of us evolves several relationship roles compiled of sets of related episodes and affective experiences, which constitute the sub-personalities of our adult self. Some of these may resemble patterns introjected from parents and significant influences, others may be reminiscent of and derived from our own childhood responses to important figures in our early lives. 'In his relationship with himself he may identify either with the parent's or the child's 'voice', and in relation to others he may enact either the parent- or the child-derived role, seeking to elicit the reciprocal role from the other' (Ryle, 1992, p. 99). My internal world will comprise a multiplicity of reciprocal roles based on millions of interactions with people, which have gradually been grouped together into particular sub-personalities or sub-selves. In my close interpersonal relationships I am likely to energise these sub-personalities in turn and project on to the other the reciprocal role, with the idiosyncratic set of expectations attached to it. Polster (1995) proposes a similar process in his discussion of self-development in the person. He holds that a person comprises 'a multiplicity of selves' all of which form part of their being in the world. He distinguishes between 'member selves' (the more peripheral aspects of self) and 'essential selves' (core senses of self) in his discussion of different experiences of self that become constellated into clusters. We in turn 'animate' these clusters by naming them 'my angry self', 'my loving self', 'my business-like self' and so on. The 'essential selves' form part of my enduring core experience of self and when such a sense of 'self' is threatened in a relationship I am likely to react strongly and protectively. Polster's position is close to that of Ryle (1992) and Karpman (1968). What Polster adds to the discussion is the concept of 'animating' the different facets of ourselves. In this sense he considers that Perls' original delineation of a 'topdog' and an 'underdog' in our intrapsychic structure constituted such an animation of experience. The advantage for the therapist in identifying the manner in which people may have 'animated' their particular self experiences is that this then opens up the way for energizing less well-recognized dimensions or activating new ones. A common challenge in therapy is to develop an 'assertive self' as distinct from an 'aggressive self'; or an 'angry self' as distinct from an 'abusive self'.

Karpman (1968), referred to above, wrote of the similarity of some of our familiar roles with those of classical drama. He describes three roles – the Persecutor, the Rescuer and the Victim – which constitute the stuff of drama and which are also seen as the easily recognizable positions we take up in our psychological games. Our internalized network of relationship dynamics will include the 'games' we learnt to play in childhood in imitation of our parents and as a way of adapting to situations where the direct expression of our needs and feelings were blocked. We have in our internal world a record of all the roles in a particular game, and when we move into Victim we will project onto the other protagonist the role of Persecutor or Rescuer, or the reverse may apply. These 'game roles' relate to fixed and repetitive patterns in our interaction with others that represent distorted efforts at communication related to unresolved issues or deficits in our early environment. They are the outward manifestations of the child's attempt to deal with the restricted or deficient conditions of the family of origin. They result from the child's attempts to deal with and protect his vulnerabilities in a less than optimal situation and constitute the best available option at the time. The nature of the game (defensive operation) will be mediated by the child's level/stage of cognitive and emotional development and the severity of the stressors operating at the time. Since even in an 'average expectable environment' there will be some shortfall, it is likely that most people will play games in their primary relationships. Berne (1964) emphasised the complementarity involved in psychological games – a game requires at least two players and both are involved in forwarding the dynamic of the game. Such games provide the couples therapist with manifest material to work with in the process of unravelling the negative interlocking pattern in the relationship linked with the internalized object relations of each partner respectively. Finding creative alternatives to game-playing may then become the primary focus of the work.

The reciprocal roles that form part of our internalized experience of relationship networks subconsciously influence the manner in which we engage with new relationships. These form the basis of the organizing principles that 'shape and thematize a person's experiences' (Stolorow and Atwood, 1992), derived from the interaction between the subjective worlds of the child and her care givers. Where a child has been subjected to extremes of reaction and experience, the roles available to her will also be polarized with very few options in the middle of the range. For example, someone who has constantly only experienced violently angry outbursts that left her feeling terrified and helpless will not have any experience of how to express anger within the middle of the range or in a way that elicits a positive outcome. Her reciprocal roles may consist of a 'captor' and a 'hostage' and these roles will affect her behaviour with a partner outside of her conscious awareness. Her partner may share a similar constellation, which interlocks with hers. Such a couple may end up in a 'captor'/'hostage' unhealthy symbiotic relationship dynamic or they may end up each competing for the power-based 'captor' position in the relationship in order to avoid feelings of powerlessness and helplessness. In either of these situations, the challenge for the couples therapist is to facilitate a middle road where each partner can be assertive without bullying, and

can be dependent without fear of being bullied. In this sense a partnership offers each of us the opportunity to find a new resolution to a
particular problem that we may carry with us as part of our repertoire
of patterns from the immediate or distant past. Such a reparative experience will lead to the evolution of new organizing principles which
will colour our behaviour and expectations in future relationships.
However, sadly, much of the time people eagerly seek on a conscious
level to break out of an archaic pattern only to end up with the very
outcome they most feared, because of deep-seated assumptions and
early conclusions about life that covertly direct their behaviour. Because of this mechanism, it becomes crucial for the brief-term couples
therapist to help partners identify dysfunctional interlocking patterns
of communication and action in order to develop more creative and
rewarding ways of being with one another. A central aim is to uncover
and facilitate the expression of healthy needs, behaviours and feelings
that may have been suppressed in the course of development so that
these can addressed in the context of the current relationship. This
process may involve giving up on deep-seated assumptions about self,
the other and relationship; for example that 'I'm unimportant and
boring'; that 'others are too busy to be interested or involved with
someone like me' and that 'relationships cannot endure beyond the
first flush of interest'. Challenging these irrational belief systems and
exposing the narrow or outdated nature of the conclusions becomes
the task of the therapist undertaking brief-term work with a couple.

Work with a couple begins at the point where the one person's world
view intersects with the other. We subscribe to an intersubjective
perspective on couples relationships, which sees interaction between
people as a dynamic ever-moving process that is influenced by a variety of factors in the current field of experience. In the therapy room,
these factors will include the person of the therapist whose very presence will affect the configuration of phenomena in the couple's immediate environment. The therapist needs to pay keen attention to his/
her contribution to the interactions generated in the session so that
these are in the service of the common agreed goals and do not insert
an intrusion of extraneous agendas into the proceedings. 'A defining
feature of our thinking lies in our not assigning any greater intrinsic
validity to the analyst's world of reality than to the patient's' (Stolorow
and Atwood, 1992, p. 206). Such a stance is predicated on giving value
to the individual and sometimes divergent views of a shared experience that emerge in the course of discussion. The therapist's view has

the advantage of providing a fresh and unbiased perspective on the couple's interaction, providing them with a mirror to reflect back incongruities and missed opportunities in their communication. Paradoxically the therapist's task is to work ourselves out of a job, so that the couple can use the skills we have contributed to their development without further input from us. In this process cognizance needs to be taken of the therapist's presence in the couple's relationship in the course of the therapy and the effects of this carefully evaluated in supervision. Although the therapist will aim to be a neutral and objective participant–observer (Sullivan, 1953), she is nevertheless a significant contributor to the process and her relationship with the couple a crucial potential healing factor for them.

THE CONCEPT OF UNCONSCIOUS 'FIT' BETWEEN PARTNERS

The idea that people may unconsciously choose partners that fit into their relationship patterns from the past has long been of interest to practitioners and theorists alike. Dicks (1993) through studying sets of spouses, noted in partners a degree of fit between their object relationship systems both at a conscious and unconscious level. He concluded that the choice of a marriage partner, though ostensibly made at a conscious level, was also largely determined by a congruence between unconscious object relations. He saw this as a desire for fit based in both conscious and unconscious processes and called it 'unconscious complementariness'. It is as though parts of the other are identified with some aspects of self:

> The sense of belonging can be understood on the hypothesis that at a deeper level there are perceptions of the partner and consequent attitudes towards him or her as if the other was part of oneself. The partner is then treated according to how this aspect of oneself was valued: spoilt and cherished, or denigrated and persecuted. (Dicks, 1993, p. 46)

This process of unconscious fit allows for partners at best to rediscover lost aspects of themselves or reintegrate denied aspects of their personalities in the course of a developing relationship. However, it can also lead to two people becoming locked in a process in which one person is resisting the re-ownership of split-off parts of the self and inducing the denied feelings in the other by a mechanism akin to projective identification. For example one person may deny any vulnerability or 'weakness' in their own make-up and define any show of neediness as a fault line in the personality. Such a person may then denigrate the neediness or helpless feelings in a spouse and persecute in the other what they will not allow in themselves. In the optimal scenario, people may well 'marry their opposites' and then proceed to learn from the other and develop in themselves some of the capacities that originally existed only in the partner. The ease with which this process unfolds may in part depend on whether the desired/admired capacity was originally associated with shame or humiliation. In such an instance it may be secretly coveted but overtly disparaged. The therapist will need to use skill and compassion in helping the person give voice to such a need in the individual's own internal make-up.

Berne (1961) who based his system on Fairbairn's theory of internal objects, called the unconscious choice of partner in marriage the 'contract of script'. He writes of this process as follows:

> The essential basis of the marriage, however, is the secret contract between two Children, the contract of script. The selection of a mate from among all the possible candidates is based on this. Each prospective spouse is in the position of a casting director. The man is seeking the lady who will best play the role cast for by the script, and the woman seeks a leading man to play the role adapted to her protocol. (Berne, 1961, p. 234)

He describes how people will then test one another out by initiating games which are played outside of Adult awareness to assess whether the other truly fits the unconscious expectations. The person will select the spouse who most clearly matches the 'script' partner sought: 'partners are drawn together by the intuitive assumption that their scripts are complementary' (Berne, 1961, p. 235). In this sense, a sleeping beauty may be waiting for a knight to awaken her, a helper may be seeking a 'less fortunate' partner to rescue from distress and some people who feel cast in the role of dependent victim may unconsciously seek out an authoritarian spouse.

The 'pull of the script' is often experienced as a compulsive attraction towards a particular person, even against one's better judgement. This can be likened to the tension of the unfinished business spoken of by gestaltists and is linked to incomplete experiences (Zeigarnik, 1927) or the unmet needs in our past. The interlocking of script patterns may lead to fixed and unhelpful patterns of interaction in which people become locked into rigid roles that limit their options and inhibit their capacity to lead a fulfilling partnership life. Since the process happens largely at the unconscious level, it will be a challenge to the brief-term couples therapist to help partners identify the point at which their scripts interlock so that they can both develop more productive communication and re-own their own denied polarities. In this sense a partnership offers each person an opportunity for a reparative experience in the present and an opportunity to extend and update their core interpersonal schema, thus leading the way to a more fulfilling relationship life.

THE CYCLE OF REINFORCEMENT OR 'VICIOUS CYCLE' OF INTERACTION

For the material in the following section, we are indebted to three principal sources: Eric Berne for his concept of the relationship diagram (Berne, 1961, p. 134); Richard Erskine for his presentation of the Interlocking Racket System (Erskine, 1982, p. 272); and Marvin Goldfried for his formulation of problematic interactions between partners (Goldfried, 1995, p. 241). These sources all supply systematic representations of the processes by which two people with different frames of reference can interlock in a manner that reinforces their underlying assumptions about themselves, others and the nature of relationship, thus forming a closed system. Goldfried and his associates have sought to frame their concepts in a common language that communicates with therapists from different orientations and attempts to provide a basis for discussion across orientations, an initiative which we applaud and support. Goldfried describes distressed marital interactions as an interpersonal 'vicious cycle' in which one person's functioning exacerbates some problematic aspects of functioning in the other, which in turn feeds back into the first person's problematic behaviour (Goldfried, 1995, p. 241). His depiction of this process involves identifying the intrapersonal and the interpersonal components of each partner's contribution to the cycle. Since this process is circular, it can start or be 'tripped off' at any point by either protagonist, or indeed by some situational variable. The process is contributed to and 'belongs to' both people; no one person is the 'cause' in any linear sense. This is a systems perspective on problematic relationship patterns.

The manner in which two people's systems may interlock is represented by Figure 1, which is of our own construction though derived from the

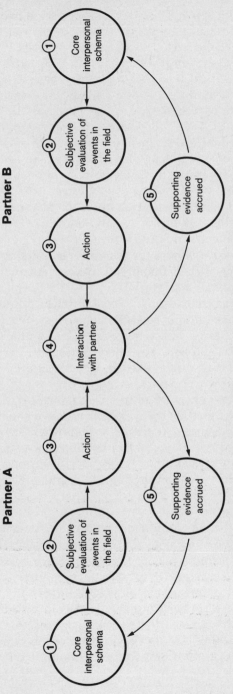

Figure 1: Cycle of reinforcement (based on Goldfried, 1995, with permission)

sources mentioned above. This interlinking process frequently operates as a closed system based on selective perception, which ends up reinforcing itself as in the 'vicious cycle' mentioned above. In that case it would be a closed system (Hall and Fagin, 1956) operating to exclude new information. In such cases, people may be heavily influenced by internal expectations not based on realistic assessment so that they screen out certain aspects of the perceptual field. The rigidity of their core interpersonal schema will influence the degree to which people are prepared to take in new, discrepant information. In open systems such a cycle will be flexible and reality-based, hence able to encompass new insights, behaviours and be available for regular revision. In these cases people will be open and aware of most forces acting upon them in a particular situation and at a given moment in time and respond in accordance with this input from the environment.

more cognitively aware of cycle

1. *Core interpersonal schema* is the person's central map of relationship containing their beliefs about self, others and the nature or possibilities of intimate relationships.
2. *Subjective evaluation of events in the field* refers to the person's emotional, cognitive and physiological responses to a particular situation; it encompasses expectations, intentions and assumptions. This process will inevitably be governed by selective perception.
3. *Action* refers to an action taken in response to the demands of an external situation or from internal imperatives.
4. *Interaction with partner* refers to an exchange between two people which may be based on the reality factors in a situation, or may be influenced by distorted, outdated or insufficient information.
5. *Supporting evidence accrued* refers to the bank of experiences of a similar nature that we store and retrieve to support our evaluation of future similar situations and use to reinforce or update our core interpersonal schema.

The diagram illustrates an interactive process whereby the assumptions and behaviours of one partner will interact with those of another in a cumulative fashion. As supporting evidence is accrued that supports particular expectations, a bank of memories is built up that a person may use to convince herself that all future interactions with her partner will have a similar consequence. He, in his turn, may well be collecting related 'evidence' that solidifies her reaction patterns. In the end, each partner may end up doing 'more of the same' (Watzlawick, Weakland and Fisch, 1974) in a frenzied attempt to effect some sort of change, yet fuelled by the anxiety that no amount of effort is ever enough to make that change happen. As long as the attempted change is pursued in the same way as in the past, the chances are very high that the 'vicious cycle' of interaction will simply be reinforced once again. The greater frequency with which this happens, the more convinced the partners become of their own perspective and the validity of their core interpersonsal schema is confirmed for them in the current relationship. Drawing up the cycle of reinforcement that operates between two people can provide the brief-term therapist with a map on which to base the interventions in the sessions. In certain cases, it has proved useful to share this 'map' with the partners or even better to ask for their help in drawing it up so that they participate in its creation. This can then lead to an exploration for healthy options which could form the basis of an alternative new 'creative map' for enhancing their relationship. The therapist needs to be sensitive in using a direct intervention of this kind so that the process is not experienced as shaming to either partner and does indeed have the desired freeing effect on their interaction.

An example of a mutual cycle of reinforcement follows. Brett has the core schema that he is unlovable, believes that others find him a burden and that his needs are 'too much for them'. He concludes that the only option is to move in and take care of others so that he can keep them around by making himself indispensable (so that he does not chase them away by revealing his own 'excessive' demands). Accordingly, when his partner withdraws from him he assumes that his needs have 'been too much for her', so he feels scared. He reacts to this fear by becoming over-attentive and parental, taking care of her in every way he can imagine to compensate for his own imagined burdensomeness to her. Jody has a core schema which suggests she is bad and selfish if she wishes to spend time on her own because others need her presence to keep them happy. She feels angry and resentful that there is no space in her current relationship to withdraw and pursue her interests. She stays around but is angry and resentful when given unwelcome 'help'. Sensing her resentment, Brett becomes more and more afraid and escalates his 'helpful' behaviours. The more helpful he is, the more resentful and 'snappy' Jody gets, thus reinforcing her belief that she is 'selfish' if she demands to be on her own for periods of time. Brett in turn concludes that he must be unlovable if she is impatient with him and tries harder to please her by being attentive and 'helpful', and so on.

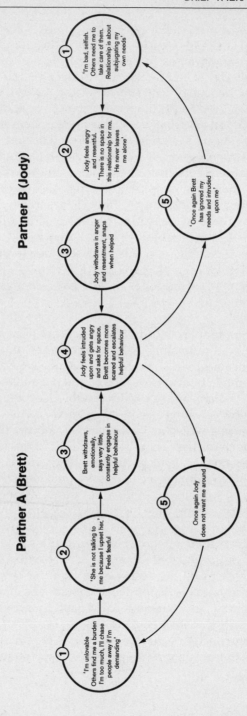

Figure 2: An example of a 'vicious cycle' of reinforcing behaviour (based on Goldfried (1995), with permission)

Berne speaks of some common styles of interaction between partners that lead to interlocking patterns that may fit the model outlined above: 'some people get along "well" together; some enjoy fighting or arguing with each other; some cannot stand each other; and some just have nothing to say to one another' (Berne, 1961, p. 137). He characterizes these styles of interaction as sympathy, antagonism, antipathy and indifference (Berne, 1961, p. 137) and believes that they are each characterized by particular styles of non-problem-solving interaction patterns (games). We have constructed examples of our own to show how two people's systems may interlock in each of these cases as follows:

1. *Sympathy*: Jean takes care of Paddy by constantly advising him and suggesting avenues of behaviour for him; this plays into Paddy's fear that he 'always messes up' if he goes it alone; the more Jean takes charge, the less faith Paddy has in his own capacities . . . ! Paddy, on the other hand, regularly gives Jean unsolicited help with her household budget, confirming for her that she 'can't manage money'. They both end up giving the other help that is unwanted and support the other's sense of incompetence in particular areas of their lives. Because of their joint fear of open disagreement and their need to please, each is too frightened to express irritation, hostility is suppressed and they are overtly solicitous and loving to one another giving the impression that they are never in conflict. Differences do not emerge and so remain unaddressed. Externally they appear to be a 'conflict-free', devoted couple.
2. *Antagonism*: Jill believes that there should be no secrets in marriage and that John should recount to her every detail of his day. Every event that he is engaged in that does not directly relate to her, she experiences as a direct rejection and an insult; consequently John tends to keep certain things to himself. Jill's aggressive verbal attacks and her expressed antipathy to John evokes his resentment and retaliation. John believes that he is entitled to keep to himself especially those matters that concern his own business interests, 'private' thoughts and 'special' friendships; as a result, he often deprives Jill of information about his feelings or about events that directly impinge upon her. His passive aggressive manner exacerbates Jill's anxiety and fuels her irritation with him. The more circumspect he becomes in his desire to preserve his privacy, the more anxious and insistent she becomes, which finds expression in her frequent attacks on him.

3. *Antipathy*: Shane feels resentful and controlled and says that his needs go unrecognized; Tracy, in turn, feels resentful and controlled by Shane's demands. Both feel that the other is demanding, un-interested in their needs and no longer loves them in the uncondi-tional way that marked their courtship. They end up competing for the other's love and attention, resenting the demands made upon them for love and care. Both of them are fixed in a position of antipathy to the other, and neither of them is prepared to budge in order to make the first move to retrieve the situation.

4. *Indifference*: Daniel is invested in attributing blame to Frances whom he sees as responsible for the breakdown of the couple's communi-cation so that he can be justified in leaving her in his own eyes and those of his friends. Frances, in turn, avoids any discussion since she does not believe that it will get them anywhere and she has long since given up hope (as has Daniel) that the situation can be re-paired. The more she withdraws, the more Daniel has a 'good case' against her; basically they are both indifferent to one another and there is very little real contact between them. They both want out, but neither wishes to be judged by society as the 'guilty' party.

INFLUENCE OF CONTEXTUAL FACTORS IN THE FIELD

In dealing with the communication patterns within couples, we do not find it useful to think in terms of linear causality. Although we do recognize the importance of the influences from the past on our current patterns of interaction, we see these as only part of the picture. In this we find ourselves aligned with Kurt Lewin's field theory of 1935, which stresses the relevance of all the factors in a person's current field of experience for understanding their behaviour: 'the cause and mean-ing of present behaviour must be sought in present dynamics, with the past as reference, but not as immediate cause' (quoted in Wheeler, 1991, p. 95). Our description of the impact of patterns derived from past experience which are carried into the present needs to be medi-ated by the influence of current factors in the field governing the couple's relationship. No one set of factors operates on its own; there are always multiple influences impacting on a couple when they arrive to seek help from the therapist.

In addition to intrapsychic and interactional factors derived from past experience, there are a multiplicity of additional forces contributing to any interactional field. These may include, *inter alia*, external circumstances such as job loss, illness, war or natural disasters, the influence of friends, cultural and class variables, economic circumstances, transport failures, the arrival of children; genetic and temperamental variables that may not be available for change; and not least, the unique intersubjective process initiated by the two people involved in the encounter. It is, therefore, crucial that the therapist explores carefully the current life situation of the couple in order to gain a picture of the forces acting upon them. Any recent changes in their context need to be noted and assessed for impact on their relationship. For example, if one partner has recently faced redundancy at work, this factor may have upset the delicate balance between the partners.

The following diagram illustrates the contextual factors operating in Rebecca and Jacques' current relationship.

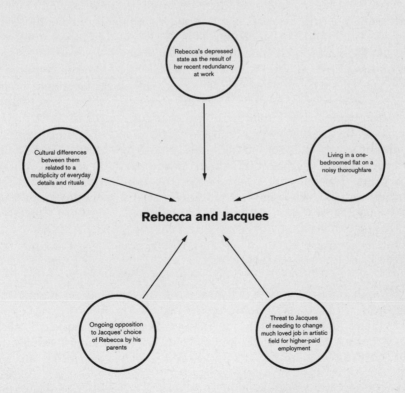

Figure 3:   Contextual factors impacting on couple relationship

The brief-term therapist is advised to draw up a diagram of this kind for the couples in his care, so that it is obvious what a multiplicity of contextual issues may be in the couple's current field of experience. If this is done together with the couple, the process can also aid them in focusing on those issues which they experience as most pressing. This will in turn help them to focus on the material to be dealt with in the sessions, since a choice of this kind sometimes from amongst several alternative possibilities will be necessary given the focused nature of the therapy.

AN INTERSUBJECTIVE PERSPECTIVE

Although the two people carry into their current relationship their characteristic ways of organizing their experience based on cumulative events, they are unique individuals in a unique new encounter with elements that will be particular to their relationship, hence too with novel possibilities for interaction. This reciprocity of mutual influence is at the heart of an intersubjective perspective in psychotherapy (Stolorow, Atwood and Brandschaft, 1994) which underlines that 'not only does the patient turn to the analyst for self object functions but the analyst also turns to the patient for such functions, although hopefully in a less archaic way' (Stolorow, Atwood and Brandschaft, 1994, p. 37). In a brief therapeutic encounter there are three sets of organising principles involved, those of the two partners and that of the therapist. As the therapist enters the couple's field of experience, they are encountering a new person, with a new perspective on relationships, and the manner in which they interact with the therapist provides immediate raw material for reflection. It is interesting to note, *inter alia*, who takes the initiative, what role is assigned to the therapist by each person, whether partners talk 'for one another', and how each defines the other's role in the relationship.

For the therapist too, there is the challenge of noting how she impacts on these two people, of being constantly alert to her own reactions, sensations, feelings and attitudes to members of the couple, to check how they are perceiving her and to be aware of counter-transference reactions that may draw her into the process. For example, a signal for added vigilance is beginning to feel sorry for one partner at the expense of the other accompanied by an aggressive attitude towards the other as the 'cause of the problem' – at such a point the therapist is probably more involved in her own agenda than open to the multiplicity of interactive factors in the couple system! If, however, as therapist you stand back and use such a counter-transference reaction as material for reflection, you may gain valuable information into the characteristic roles taken by each person where one may be the 'victim' and the other cast as the 'persecutor' in their relationship drama.

In conclusion, our model can be described as an integrative approach to working with couples from an intersubjective perspective that takes into account the factors currently acting upon the couple as well as the influence of internalized relationship patterns from the past. In the course of the succeeding chapters we will demonstrate some ways of intervening that we have found effective in brief therapy with couples. We will illustrate our approach in the case study of Grant and Jessica, which shows the interplay between learnt patterns of interaction from the past with factors currently impacting on their relationship. We will also make some practical suggestions about homework exercises related to the themes covered in the chapters.

4

ASSESSMENT AND PROBLEM DEFINITION

From the initial assessment, the couples therapist will derive a picture of the relationship along several dimensions which we will outline below. The therapist will hope to gain a sense of areas of strength and areas of deficit in the relationship. The aim of this initial assessment is for all parties to arrive at a shared formulation of the problem that can lead to joint goal-setting. Such a shared goal is essential to brief-term treatment. Because brief-term therapy is by its very nature limited in scope, the process of choosing and focusing on a goal that is manageable within the time frame is already an important facet of the therapeutic endeavour. Where such a shared goal is not possible because of widely divergent needs and perceptions of the situation, the therapist may agree to spend the therapy sessions exploring these discrepancies with the couple in order to establish whether there is a possible way forward for them or not as the case may be. This project will then become the focus of the initial six-to-eight session intervention.

At the outset there are a few questions that may help the therapist to focus in on the couple's relationship and what his own role will be in the sessions:

- Why now? It is important to establish the immediately precipitating cause for the request for therapy. Why have these two people come seeking help at this particular juncture, and what is the significance of the predisposing factors that have brought them to the therapist's rooms? An answer to this question will give the therapist a sense of the expectations and of the current focus of the people involved. The precipitating cause, e.g. the termination of a pregnancy or the loss of a job by one partner, will be impacting the two in very different ways. There has often been some crisis that impels people to seek help, whereas they may have been enduring discomfort for some time and 'meaning to phone'. From asking this question the therapist will almost certainly gain a rapid view of the presenting issues.

- What expectations?   The therapist would do well to check out the couple's expectations of therapy, as well as their perception of how this process is to take place. Sometimes people come with fairly detailed and realistic expectations based on 'our friends who went to one of your colleagues' or on their reading, whereas others may be looking to the therapist to do the work for them or perform some magic to help them recover their courtship experience.

- Why me or why this particular context?   It can be helpful to know why the couple has sought to contact you for therapy. Answers may be illuminating and helpful/informative in a variety of ways: 'We want brief-term couples therapy and we've heard that's what you offer'; 'We wanted to see your colleague but she didn't have space so she referred us to you – we do hope that you are as good as she is!'; 'We consulted the register and found your name among the therapists in our area'. The hopes, wishes, regrets or fears expressed in response to this question can be dealt with right at the outset of the work so that they do not undermine the process of the therapy through remaining unexpressed. A crucial factor in successful therapy is the faith that people have that the therapist can actually help them. If there is any information about the therapist's training and/or experience that will help them in this regard, it can be supplied at this point. The couple may also have had special reasons for seeking therapy in the context in which you work. For example, Sharon and James had been very scared of approaching a couples therapist, but when their general practitioner referred them to the counsellor recently employed to work at the practice, they felt more contained by the familiar context.

The partners that comprise the couple will bring to the sessions their own characteristic ways of relating, problem-solving and expressing intimacy and love for one another. We base our assessment on a relationship analysis of this process, that focuses on several dimensions of the communication between two people. The schema of relationship dimensions presented below represents an integration of concepts derived from Berne (1961), Boyd and Boyd (1981), Goldfried (1995) and our own extensive clinical experience with couples. We will also be presenting an assessment model that looks at the different developmental stages of the couples relationship to provide the therapist with an additional perspective for understanding the dynamics of the underlying pattern that may be operating at a particular phase. The aim of this assessment is to help the therapist to focus on the central problem areas, to consider what needs to be achieved and to consider what his own role will be in the healing process. Such a detailed and specific assessment procedure enables the therapist to target areas for change which will assist in the effective formulation of the therapeutic contract with the couple. In brief-term therapy the assessment process is crucial to effective outcomes. It is only with a clear contract and a well-defined set of goals that the therapist and the couple can make the best use of the time frame. That way all three parties have a clear picture from the outset what their business together is about and what results they are hoping to achieve in the sessions.

RELATIONSHIP DIMENSIONS FOR ASSESSMENT AND PROBLEM FORMULATION WITH COUPLES

We will now describe a series of relationship dimensions that form the basis for assessment. The couple is assessed in terms of each of these to establish where the major stuck point/s occur in the relationship. We will follow this in the latter part of the book with a detailed outline of each of these dimensions and discuss strategies for intervention into each specific dimension. The primary questions that the therapist will be answering in the course of the assessment are these:

- In what relationship dimension is the primary problem located?
- How do each of these people characteristically constellate their experience of relationship?
- What meaning do they attribute to what happens between them?
- What can I as therapist do to help these two people remedy this problem?
- What particular strengths do each of these two people already possess that may assist them in this process of problem resolution?
- What particular interventions, exercises and homework assignments will be of best assistance to this couple in the course of a brief-term therapy?
- Does a knowledge of the developmental stage of their relationship throw any light on an understanding of their presenting issue?

Exceptions
Scaling
miracle question

Compatibility of Value Systems, Core Beliefs and Frames of Reference

Do the partners share common values and assumptions about priorities? People's value systems will determine how they spend their time and money, how they treat their nearest and dearest, their attitudes to child-rearing, to friendship, to the extended family, to work, to worship, and what they are prepared to die for. Boyd and Boyd (1981) suggest that for two people to be compatible the general ordering of their values must be similar. 'In a compatible couple the partners are in general agreement about the relative importance of issues such as play, money, work, sex, intimacy, alone time, family, child management and friends' (Boyd and Boyd, 1981). Although in general agreement with the sentiment ex-pressed here, we would add that an agreement to differ on certain counts and to respect such diversity in a partner can form the basis for a fruitful relationship where such differences are openly acknowledged and negotiated. In cross-cultural partnerships, differences in value systems often need to be negotiated at the outset because they stand out in sharp relief. Writers in the field have identified several di-mensions along which partners in a cross-cultural relationship may differ e.g. individualism–collectivism; independence–interdependence; competition–cooperation (Brown and Landrum-Brown, 1995). Couples who share a common culture usually implicitly assume that there is agreement on matters of value, priorities and basic assumptions about life. Differences tend subsequently to come into sharp relief in the course of the first few years of the partnership. In their initial presentation, couples usually refer to or display disagreements about values in what each of them chooses to emphasize as the problem area. 'We just can't agree about the children . . .', 'We never talk to one another . . .', 'I don't want to visit her family every holiday . . .'. This will give the therapist immediate access to the different priorities of the partners and to the disagreements that may have acted as a catalyst for their arrival in his rooms.

More generally a person's frame of reference (Schiff *et al.*, 1975) governs the way the person perceives, experiences and defines the world and everything in it. Each of us will experience the world in our own subjec-tive way, but in our shared world find enough common ground to negotiate mutual goals. However, if people differ very widely about the way they structure reality, they may continually disagree about the very nature of 'reality' as each perceives it. For example, they may constantly

need to have similar ground when constructing reality

disagree about what happened, whether certain events happened at all or who said or did what to whom, and with what consequences. Such basic disagreements at the level of 'perceived reality' may render couples work extremely difficult or even impossible, unless there is a willingness on both sides to develop an understanding and appreciation of the other's world view. If two people appear to be competing about who has the right to define their joint reality, the therapist may be learning something important about the power base in the relationship.

Effectiveness of Problem-solving and Conflict Resolution

In this regard the couples therapist will be assessing the couple's effectiveness at dealing with the organisation of their everyday lives and at dealing with conflict as this arises between them. Relevant questions for the therapist to explore follow below.

- Are these two people able to discuss practical matters and run their home efficiently?
- Do these two people respect one another's opinions and input into discussions?
- How do they handle shared resources?
- Can they parent their children safely, lovingly and effectively?
- When they disagree, do they have efficient and supportive ways available to them to resolve conflict? How do they make decisions?
- Is power shared in this regard, or does one person tend to take the lead? And how does the other partner regard this process?
- Are both partners able to listen to the other and appreciate a different point of view? How is anger expressed?
- Are the partners able to be assertive without resorting to angry attacks and/or physical violence?

What we are assessing here is whether the two people in the partnership have sufficient maturity to allow them to listen to, respect and respond to the other's opinions, suggestions and analyses of events so that they can make mutually satisfactory decisions about the ongoing concerns in their lives. We are aware here that we adhere to a value that mutuality and sharing in decision-making are important ingredients in a well-functioning relationship. This value may be given a different weight in different cultures or sub-cultures, depending on prevailing norms about authority and the manner in which power is exercised. For example, in a culture where collectivism and the extended family play a significant part in the daily lives of everyone, decision-making may rest in the hands of the 'elders'.

This dimension will then be taken into account in the process of assessment, the object of which is to describe the problem areas that people experience themselves, not to define for them what we think they should change in terms of our own frames of reference.

Emotional Intimacy, Capacity to Have Fun and to Achieve Sexual Gratification

Here the couples therapist will be assessing the partners' capacity to engage in spontaneous contact. Relevant questions to be explored would include the following:

- Do these two people express their emotions to one another?
- Do they express affection, anger, joy, fear, sadness and the wealth of emotion available to us as human beings? Or is their range of emotional expression restricted or virtually absent?
- Do they have fun together?
- Do they 'play' and share moments of humour and relaxation?
- Do they have any shared leisure activities and interests?
- Do they communicate their wishes, hopes, dreams and disappointments with one another?
- Do they have a mutually satisfactory sexual relationship? If not, what is the nature of the problem?
- If sexual contact is not happening, how do both parties feel about this, and how do they explain it?
- Do they enjoy intimate moments of intense contact, the I–Thou contact so eloquently described by Buber (1994)?

We wish to acknowledge that we are making the assumption that intimacy is a vital component in a mutually fulfilling relationship and see the capacity to 'play' as the third element in Freud's often quoted definition of health 'to love and to work' (Freud, quoted in Erikson, 1950). This basic need for relationship underlies our approach and informs the work that we do with couples. However, we do not see it as our task to prescribe how people are intimate together or the degree or extent of that intimacy. The relevant issue here is whether each member of the couple is satisfied with the intimacy between them and if not, where the remedy lies.

Caring for the Other, Giving Support, Warmth and Succour in Times of Need

This dimension refers both to a basic level of care for another human being's survival needs and to a capacity for warm, supportive nurturing of another.

On the very basic level the couples therapist will establish whether these two people are respectful of each other's survival needs? Is there any danger to children in this home? If there is physical or psychological violence in the relationship, if either person's safety is at stake, if there is abusive behaviour on either part, if one person is depriving the other of food, medical care or any of the other basic necessities of life, then this criterion is not being met. We are referring here to the very basic level of care that any of us in a civilized world have the right to expect from any other person we come into contact with in our everyday life. If there is a deficit in this level of care in a relationship, then this needs to be attended to first before any other intervention is considered. In fact, where abuse is happening at this level, the couples therapist may find that another style of intervention needs to happen in conjunction with couples therapy.

The second level of caring refers to each partner's capacity to be warm and lovingly supportive to the other in times of need, to display a parental function towards the other when that person is sick, down, tired and in need of care. We believe that this capacity for caring is an important bedrock for a relationship and at its best will be manifest in a loving and caring consideration of the other in daily life, not solely in times of extremity. It will manifest in the consideration partners give to one another in the ongoing fabric of their shared lives.

Relevant questions here include:

● Can these two people support the other in his/her dependency? Or is the expectation that the other should be 'strong' and not need succour or support?

- Does each person give the other warm support and care in times of need – when the other is weighed down, suffering, ill, depleted or otherwise not in a position to engage in the full mutuality of relationship?
- Is this type of warm care extended at other times as a spontaneous expression towards the other?
- Does this supportive function extend to giving extra help at times when one partner is carrying a heavier burden of responsibility than the other?

Assessing the level of awareness of the 'problem' as experienced by self and other:

At this level, the couples therapist is observing the presentation of the couple as a unit and assessing the extent to which there is a mutual understanding and agreement about the central problem/desired area for growth in the relationship. The aim at this assessment stage is to arrive at a shared formulation of the problem that can lead to joint goal-setting. If the partners cannot agree on what they wish to change and do differently, then the therapy as such may not be able to proceed until shared goals can be agreed. By this we mean a basic agreement that both partners wish to work on the relationship and that they have a shared sense of a conceivable and realizable change that they both wish to attain.

Questions that are relevant here include:

- Do the partners agree about what they wish to attain between them? Do they share a picture of their aimed-for relationship?
- Do these two people agree about the nature of the problem between them, or do they discount the significance of what is distressing the other?
- Do there appear to be areas that are never spoken about to the other?
- If there is a conspiracy of silence in any particular area, how does this affect the two people differentially?
- If they consider that they have a communication problem, who is defined as 'owning' it?

The aim at this point is to assess the nature of problem description and definition between the partners. We may find that responsibility is either avoided, assumed overly much or displaced. For example: 'It's her fault, she simply won't listen to me at all, she's so selfish'; 'I know it's really my fault, I feel very guilty about all the ways that I have failed my partner'; 'I always knew marriage was an impossible institution and this just proves it, how can you expect two people to live cheek by jowl for years on end in any sort of harmony?' Joint ownership of a problem and an agreed definition of the problem are the basic building blocks for effective short-term work.

Finally, the couples therapist will be in a position to pull together all the threads from the relationship dimensions outlined above. This will give a picture of the extent and type of contact that these two people are maintaining and show up the deficits in communication. These deficits and their potential remedies will then form the focus of the brief-term therapy.

In our experience one or two of these dimensions feature prominently in the assessment and guide the goal-setting process. These foci then help the therapist and the couple to formulate the specific contract(s) for the brief-term intervention.

USING A DEVELOPMENTAL MODEL TO ASSESS THE STAGE OF THE RELATIONSHIP

> Just as the individual has a life cycle, so too do a couple and a family. A couple and family are units continually adapting to new situations and crises by modifying their structure. For example, no change is so profound as the emergence of a third person out of a couple, and the birth of a child profoundly and permanently alters the nature of a couple. (Jaffe and Viertal, 1979, p. 186)

The therapist can use a developmental model for purposes of assessment, both to focus on the life stage of each partner and to look at the stage of development of the relationship as a separate entity. An early and still influential approach to human development is Erikson's (1950) description of the three stages of adulthood in his view of the lifespan. He characterises the first task of adulthood as establishing intimacy. Where there is failure in this regard, he talks about isolation. We see the basic task of the family as needing to provide for the development of its members. When it stops working at this task, it begins to disintegrate and family members begin to show pathological

symptoms. In the case of couples, they will begin to manifest difficulties. The establishment of intimacy rests on a firm sense of identity
which Erikson describes as culminating in adolescence (Erikson, 1950).
Our perspective is that the development of a sense of identity begins in
early childhood and strongly rests on the successful negotiation and
balancing of processes of separation and individuation (Mahler *et al.*,
1975), as these are mediated by the norms of a particular culture. The
emphasis that we in the western world place on individualism and
early independence from the family of origin as signs of psychological
health is not shared, for instance, by African and Arabic cultures where
loyalty to the extended family remains a priority throughout life. For
this reason, we need to look at separation–individuation in relation to
the norms of the particular culture that has mediated the process.
Differences on this level are particularly noticeable in cross-cultural
marriages where the two people involved may place different demands on the children or where the independence of one partner is
viewed by the other as a betrayal of loyalty and love.

In the modern world, we observe that adults are constantly negotiating
identity and intimacy issues. Although Erikson's theory places the
negotiation of identity as a crisis to be resolved at adolescence, followed by the intimacy crisis, the complexity of modern life and the
breakdown of traditional family values and roles throws people into
renegotiating these issues at various points in their adulthood. This
process will inevitably impact on their relationships. Many young
people form relationships and/or marry in order to find their identities. This has been particularly true of women who often have experienced the pressure to become wives and mothers first in order to find
themselves as people. The widespread occurrence of divorce with relationships ending or breaking up also has a significant effect on identity. Losing status as a wife or husband causes a sense of the loss of
aspects of the self and hence a change in the core sense of self identity.
In the course of an intimate relationship with a partner, much of our
identity will be influenced and shaped by our interactions with this
chosen person. As our sense of self is continually updated and co-
created in our close relationships, a breakdown in a partnership can
have devastating effects on a person's self-concept. It is not unusual for
partners in a divorce, whether they have initiated the process or not, to
entertain suicidal ideation and on occasion to act upon it. The loss of a
close and important person in our lives, whether by death or divorce,
is often experienced as 'losing part of myself' or 'I feel lost and

incomplete'. A person 'bereaved' in this way will need time for the gradual reconstruction of a viable sense of identity, particularly as this impacts on intimate relationships. This trauma will inevitably colour subsequent partnerships, as is demonstrated in our case example.

In an interesting model Bader and Pearson (1988) use the stages of early development outlined by Mahler *et al.* (1975) as descriptions and metaphors of the process couples go through in the course of their partnership history. They use their model both for diagnosis and treatment planning. We think it is important to accept this as a metaphor and a description rather than as a fact. Clearly, however, relationships of any length will go through a developmental process and the stages they describe have some clinical relevance for couples work. This theory is to some extent culture-bound and for this reason may have less relevance to partnerships in other cultures or cross-culturally. However, we have found that they provide a perspective that has proved useful to some couples for understanding the sudden emergence of tensions between them that result from changes in their respective relationship needs and requirements. There may indeed be recognizably distinct phases in relationship that can be traced in different cultures and sub-cultures that pertain to a particular culture or sub-grouping. For example, we have mentioned earlier that remarried couples often seek help sooner in the relationship than first-time couples because they are more aware of the need for 'working on' a relationship. This may also mean that the initial phase of the relationship has a different flavour and tone.

Bader and Pearson's model draws heavily on the work of Mahler *et al.* (1975) which they transpose from the early development of the child to the progressive stages of the couple's relationship. Such a transposition will have some limiting aspects because the needs for partners may not be strictly in accordance with those of the developing child. However, there are useful insights to be gained from this perspective if it is viewed more as a metaphor rather than too literally interpreted.

The Symbiotic Phase

The earliest phase, the so-called 'falling in love' or 'honeymoon phase' is described as the symbiotic phase. Margaret Mahler saw this as the early bonding phase between mother and child and the very beginnings of the

child's experience of relationship. This phase is crucial to the establishment of bonding and affectional ties. At this stage couples look for the
similarities, emphasize the sameness and avoid the differences between
them. Where they receive nurturance from each other and agree to form
a couple, a good foundation in attachment allows them to move forward
to a differentiating phase. When this initial phase is not successfully
established, the couple will remain symbiotically connected presenting
with two possible forms of dysfunction: one, enmeshment characterized
by merger and avoidance of conflict; or two, hostile-dependency, 'the
hostile-dependent system is dominated by anger and conflict. Too terrified to end the relationship, and not mature enough to end the battles,
the couple remain locked in endless rounds of mutually inflicted pain'
(Bader and Pearson, 1988, p. 10). This relationship is characterized by 'I
can't live with you, and I can't live without you'. On the other hand,
couples who remain enmeshed may do so at the cost of the individual
development of one of the partners who may submerge personal needs
completely to the relationship demands. Any conflict or difference is
minimized and the couple function as a merged unit without a sense of
their separate identities: 'Your wish is my wish'.

The Differentiation Phase

A natural next phase after the bonding is the stage of differentiating
out as distinct individuals. As differences emerge, some of the early
idealization dissipates. Partners frequently start wanting space and
wish to re-establish their own boundaries. It is important for the couples therapist to bear in mind that this is a familiar process supported
by western cultural values and to normalize for the couple their need
to individuate. This can often be a painful process for people who find
that their initial assumption that the other person is in perfect agreement with them on most matters was really a comfortable illusion
fostered by both at the outset when in the 'honeymoon phase'. The task
of the couple's therapist will be to assist people in acknowledging and
expressing their differences. Partners will then need to negotiate a
different way of relating that involves a respect for separate individual
needs which require expression within the wider frame of the relationship. If either partner has strong unresolved issues related to abandonment, the couple may become stuck at this phase, with one in a state of
constant fear of abandonment, whilst the other feels hemmed in and
constrained by demands to remain symbiotic.

The Practising Phase

The differentiation phase is succeeded by the practising phase. The practising phase of early development is described by Mahler *et al.* as one where the child's cognitive and physical abilities are rapidly leading the child to explore the world for herself with interest and excitement (Mahler *et al.*, 1975). Differentiation is followed by practising, in which there is an even further distancing from each other. Couples may stop being attuned to each other and direct their attention to autonomy and individuation. This usually coincides with the advent of children and the rapid career development characterized by longer periods at work or frequent travelling on the part of either or both partner. At this stage in the relationship, partners begin to explore their own individual interests and may seek personal and professional development that takes them in separate directions from one another. As the novelty of the relationship has begun to fade, the partners may feel less inclined to spend time alone with one another to consolidate other aspects of their life or build up new shared interests. This is often identified as a lack when they present for therapy.

The Rapprochement Phase

When there is a well-developed sense of identity, the partners can afford to become more emotionally vulnerable to each other once again. This next phase, the rapprochement, is characterized by alternating expressions of increased intimacy and increased independence in the young child, and consequently also in the couple according to this model. It provides the adult partners with the opportunity to resolve earlier issues of closeness versus abandonment, or the fear of engulfment. A resolution of this process would allow for a mutually enriching and enhancing relationship in which there is both security and containment, as well as the opportunity for personal development and extension. When partners present at this stage, they are usually faced with renegotiating their closeness whilst not sacrificing their individual needs and interests that may not be so readily supplied within the boundary of the relationship. Resentments may also have built up over the years of independent 'practising', especially if one partner feels 'left behind' by the other's pursuits and career development or 'left out from' an independent friendship circle. At this stage the task for the couple is to 'come back together' in a new way so that they can both enjoy intimacy and maintain their own sense of individuality.

We now conclude with a brief summary of the various stages outlined by Bader and Pearson (1988), demonstrating how these can combine in different configurations since development in the partners is not always evenly matched. One partner can be at a particular stage of development in the relationship process, whilst the other is at an earlier or later stage. If such discrepancies are present, there will be an inevitable conflict of needs and interests as people experience being 'out of step' with one another. Many couples who come for help will entertain conflicting views of their current image of a desirable and fulfilling relationship. If these views can be related to this model, people sometimes experience relief that what they are facing has been identified and described by others. The model also points to issues that can be addressed in the course of the therapy. The following summary can serve as a useful checklist for the brief-term therapist during the assessment process with a couple.

Symbiotic–symbiotic: (Enmeshed – 'we are one')

This is the 'falling in love' bonding stage which establishes the 'coupleness'. This stage is characterized by closeness and the assumption of similarity. The stalemates include loss of individuality, fear of abandonment and passivity. The primary treatment intervention involves facilitating differentiation and helping people realize that the presence of conflict or anger is not to be equated with loss of love.

Symbiotic–symbiotic (Hostile–dependent – 'I can't live with you, and I can't live without you'.)

This is a manifestation of the bonding stage which is particularly problematic. This kind of relationship commonly presents for help and is one of the most challenging for the therapist in that it emerges as the symbiotic fantasy begins to fade. It is characterized by open and often angry expressions of anger, bitterness and blame. The major therapeutic goal is to contain conflict and help partners develop a vision of a better future. Partners stuck at this stage are usually struggling with fears of abandonment which are in conflict with desires for independence. The other is blamed both for desertion in times of need and simultaneously for not supporting the other's desires for some independence from the relationship. This ambivalence results directly from the unsuccessful resolution of the separation-individuation process in childhood and adolescence.

Symbiotic–differentiating – 'Don't betray me'

One of the partners starts on a differentiating process while the other is clinging or resisting separation. The main task is learning to risk expressing difference. The problem is the imbalance and the fear of betrayal, while the differentiating partner feels anger and guilt. The help partners need is with differentiating, respecting difference and tolerating anger. The 'clinging' partner may be faced with the task of developing greater self-reliance and trust in his own judgement, whereas the 'differentiating' partner may need to learn how to balance remaining caring and intimate with the desire for exploration.

Differentiating–differentiating – 'I'll change if you change'

Here both partners are struggling to manage differences. They need to learn to fight successfully. As Wile says: 'The general orientation recommended here is to help fighting partners to fight,' (Wile, 1981, p. 176). Partners may need assistance from the therapist in learning the rules that govern fair fighting, e.g. to stay with one issue at a time. Helping partners articulate feelings is central to treatment at this stage, as well as facilitating the differentiation process both from the family of origin, if appropriate or desired, and in their couple relationship.

Symbiotic–practising – 'Don't leave me, leave me alone'

Once partners are two stages apart, the issues get exaggerated. While the symbiotic partner longs for merger and fears abandonment, feeling betrayal and attempting to intensify the enmeshment, the practising partner has lost empathy for the other's need and tries to escape the engulfment. Treatment here focuses on clarifying discrepant goals, helping the symbiotic partner to become more self-directed and the practising partner to re-engage empathically. In this case, the child-hood intrapsychic conflicts may need to be addressed for a successful resolution to ensue.

Practising–practising – 'I want to be me'

These relationships are characterized by power struggles and the fear that 'greater intimacy will lead to loss of self' (Bader and Pearson, 1988, p. 249). Treatment focuses on the process rather than content of the conflicts. Here, too, partners will be resolving childhood issues and developing a decision-making process. Although turbulent, the fights between the partners are more accessible to resolution than the earlier hostile–dependent expressions of anger. The advantage in this instance is that both people are facing similar challenges in the relationship and are therefore more likely to have empathy with one another's dilemma. Problems at this stage may be the ever-widening gulf between the two as they travel their individual paths; or a competitive stance 'I will reach out, if you do!'

Practising – Rapprochement – 'One foot in, one foot out'

The partner in the rapprochement phase is wanting to return to the intimacy and emotional sustenance of the relationship. There is the re-emergence of vulnerability with greater ease of negotiating. The treatment goals primarily involve finding a way of balancing both sets of needs, since one partner is still seeking to establish a separate sense of self.

Rapprochement–rapprochement – 'Homeward bound'

At this stage, there is a realignment between the partners who are now re-engaging in an intimate way as separate individuated people. Since each now has a clearly established sense of personal identity, they are not threatened by closeness and shared activities. At this advanced stage in a relationship the stresses usually come from external sources rather than from tensions within the relationship. Therapy is primarily facilitative rather than treatment-oriented. However, if the couple has encountered a sudden and traumatic life stress, the brief-term intervention may involve dealing with the effects of post-traumatic stress in one or both partners.

This brief summary of Bader and Pearson's interesting model gives an idea as to the usefulness of locating couples in terms of each partner's position on a separation–individuation continuum. The earlier or less differentiated the couples are, the more difficult they are to work with as the struggles are intense and usually involve unresolved childhood issues as well. Bader and Pearson's work contains much that is useful in terms of treatment techniques as well as an understanding of the dynamics involved. What we have given here is a brief overview of the main stages presented by Bader and Pearson. In diagnosing a couple, they recognize the validity of all these possible combinations, each with their own particular strengths and problem areas. In checking through these options, the brief couples therapist can identify the stage of the particular relationship and be alerted to possible conflicts, needs and styles of relating characteristic of the stage.

For the brief-term couples therapist, such a developmental perspective of the relationship can facilitate the understanding of their process by the partners. This allows the therapist to reframe their struggles, for example, as moves towards individuation and separateness, while at the same time not wanting to lose the security, contact and closeness of the relationship. It can be reassuring for the partners to recognize that other couples too tend to experience a developmental sequence and in that sense they are not unique in their struggles. This can have a normalizing effect.

CONTRAINDICATIONS FOR BRIEF THERAPY WITH COUPLES

The Presence of Severe Personality Problems

A contraindication for brief therapy with a couple may be the presence of severe personality problems in one or both partners leading to defective caring and a lack of respect at a basic human level (e.g. violence, frequent abuse etc.) that constantly undermines the very survival of one or both people and the children involved. A different intervention, e.g. by Social Services, may be more relevant. However, if the partners are open and willing to change and immediately cease the abusive behaviours, then a brief intervention in conjunction with other types of support may well be effective in pointing a new direction. Our experience suggests that longer-term couples therapy may be more effective in such cases, combined with individual therapy for one or both partners if this is at all feasible in terms of resources.

Fragmentation of Experience of Self

A severe fragmentation of the sense of self in one partner which leads to an inability really to see or respect the other as a separate person in their own right would also be a contraindication for a brief-term intervention with a couple. The model we use assumes a capacity for self-reflection and the ability to view oneself as an element in a partnership duo. If, therefore, one or both partners have not developed an 'observing ego' (Sterba, 1934), which allows them to stand back from and assess their own behaviour in relation to others, our approach to brief therapy will not 'take'. We are assuming that couples who come to us may well exhibit some difficulty with this process because of embedded assumptions and set ways of viewing their experience. However, it is the capacity for observing self in action and the ability for self-reflection that are crucial for change.

Lack of Good Will, Indifference, Energies Invested Elsewhere

Sometimes couples present for therapy with a distinct lack of good will towards one another and regard the therapist rather as the 'judge' who will express sentence on their relationship than as a facilitator of change. More common is the situation where one partner still retains the good will towards the other and the desire to work on the relationship, whereas the other has long since lost any investment in and commitment to the process. Such a person may come along to therapy to 'be seen' to do the right thing by society and family, but really have no interest in the process of therapy nor any intention to change. In some instances, one partner is already involved in another intimate relationship where her/his energies are invested and no longer has the emotional investment in the original partnership. Such mixed motives do not augur well for brief-term therapy with couples which has as its premise the investment and interest of both parties to achieve a common relationship goal. The authors have on occasion in such instances agreed on a contract to work with the couple on their separation and effecting this in a way that impacts least destructively on one another and the children (where a family is involved in the process). Such 'divorce' or 'separation' therapeutic work falls well within the brief of the couples therapist engaged in brief-term intervention. A creative process of disengagement may well be the joint goal desired by the partners!

5

CONTRACTING IN BRIEF THERAPY WITH COUPLES

We define a contract as a mutual agreement linked to specific goals that are agreed upon by all the parties involved: each person in the couple and the therapist. The importance of the contract lies in the adult-to-adult nature of this negotiation, in which each protagonist takes responsibility for ensuring the outcome (Berne, 1966). In this sense there is ownership of a common goal by all three people involved – the couple to work with good will towards the shared relationship goals and the therapist to facilitate this process and contribute to it his/her knowledge, skill and therapeutic presence.

Neutrality on the part of the therapist is crucial to the success of couples work, and more especially where only six to eight sessions are involved. It is important that the therapist clearly define his role – that he is there as a facilitator, to act as a 'mirror' for the couple, to reflect on the process he observes, to offer 'experiments' that can lead to better contact between people and to monitor 'homework' assignments that have been agreed. His role is not to act as a judge or arbiter of reality to decide that one person's view is 'right' and the other therefore by definition 'wrong'. We see the main process objective of brief-term therapy with couples to enable a greater understanding between two people of the other's frame of reference. An essential part of the contracting process is the clarification of the therapist's role in relation to the expectations that the partners have of him. The therapist will also need to outline the parameters of brief-term therapy so that the clients understand the limitations and the possible gains of this approach to couple's work.

A respect for the multiple diversity of human experience and different frames of reference underpins our practice. We do not believe that there is any one way of having a good relationship; in our experience, there are many and varied successful and functional models of being in relationship with another. For this reason, it is crucial that the contract agreed by the participants comes out of their need and can be agreed as important by them, rather than that the therapist defines what they 'should' be achieving. If the therapist is at any time in conflict with her own values and those of the couple in a way that prevents her from delivering an effective service, then this is better declared and the couple referred elsewhere. The people in our care have the right to our unfettered attention in the process of our work with them. Regular supervision of the couples therapist's work goes some way to ensuring that our own prejudices and assumptions about ideal relationships, our cultural beliefs about what constitutes an effective relationship, or our biases about relationship possibilities, do not lead us to impose these, albeit subtly, upon others.

AGREEING OBJECTIVES AND MAKING A FORMAL THERAPEUTIC CONTRACT

In the assessment session (preceding a six-to-eight session series) the chief goal is for the therapist and each partner to agree on common objectives and to make a formal therapeutic contract for the period of therapy. These goals are briefly reviewed at the beginning of each session to keep the participants focused on the agreed task. The contract is the vehicle for choosing and keeping a focus for the period unless at any point there is a renegotiation and the contract is reviewed and changed. Such a pointed focus on a particular goal(s) is one of the chief characteristics of a brief-term intervention. The therapist is also bound by this agreement and not at liberty to range into other areas of concern except in so far as these are deemed to relate to the central focus. This, however, does not inhibit the therapist from highlighting other areas of work in the course of the six-to-eight session period for future consideration. On occasion the contract may be reviewed and changed or refined in the light of information that has emerged in the course of the sessions. In this sense, the protagonists are not enslaved by the contract, rather it serves the purpose of focusing and containment for the therapeutic process. However, therapists engaged in brief-term work report that it takes self-control to focus in this way, because of the attraction and interest in avenues of possible exploration that open up along the way as the sessions progress. The therapist needs to keep a tight reign on any agenda of his own which may conflict with the immediate and best interests of his clients in their agreed focus.

The focused nature of this work distinguishes it from many forms of longer-term therapy which can be more exploratory and open. For this reason, brief-term therapy may not suit all temperaments since it requires a sharp focus, targeted interventions into the relationship process and then a withdrawal from involvement in the couple's system all within a relatively short time-frame. A therapist who had engaged in this type of work for some years reported: 'I am getting drained by this constant process of saying hello and goodbye in such a short time-band. I engage intensely with people, work at a deep and intimate level with them and then they are gone and the next couple appears. I know the process works but I am left with too many goodbyes . . .'.

A focus on a contracted task does not mean an inattention to the process between the partners and between them and the therapist. Since the focus of the contract is generally on some specific aspect of the process of interaction between the partners or will very soon emerge as such even if the contract is about 'getting assistance in making a decision to . . .', the distinction between content and process is not of particular relevance. It is the dysfunctional nature (in their particular context) of certain patterns of interaction between people that usually underpins whatever unresolved conflicts or specific content areas bring them to therapy. On p. 72 we will distinguish between intrapyschic process contracts and contracts for specific behavioural change, which we see as a set of inter-related goals in therapy.

BUSINESS CONTRACT

The business contract involves agreements about fees, frequency and venue for meetings, times and length of sessions, and the total number of sessions. We recommend six to eight sessions; this does not usually include the assessment/goal-setting session. The last or sometimes the penultimate session would serve as an evaluation and review of gains made and would also involve any recommendations for the future. On occasion couples may return for another series of sessions in six months or a year's time. This will then be negotiated at that time with the therapist.

We wish briefly to discuss the question of the frequency of sessions. In our experience a two-week interval between sessions has proved to be the most beneficial. This gives the couple enough time to process what has emerged in the session without losing the momentum of the therapy. This time frame also allows for enough space for homework assignments to be put into practice by the couple, their results evaluated and the effects felt. As regards session length, 1½ hours seems most productive. This gives enough time for a brief review of the situation thus far, time to work on the contracted focus and a brief period at the end of the session for summing up and coming to an agreement about any 'homework' or further specific contracts between the partners that have grown out of the particular session.

INTRAPSYCHIC PROCESS CONTRACTS AND CONTRACTS FOR SPECIFIC BEHAVIOURAL CHANGES

We distinguish two levels of the contract made in brief-term therapy which are linked with one another in the work. Contracts for specific behavioural changes grow out of the focus on problem areas in the relationship. Such behavioural changes inevitably involve the need for internal intrapsychic process change as well to support and facilitate the development of new behaviour patterns. Most couples who come for help have already 'tried' all their current known options for behaviour, so the issue is seldom one of simply suggesting new behaviours. The intrapsychic process that underpins the interlocking process needs to be investigated and understood. The dynamics of this process have been extensively discussed in Chapter 3. Sometimes long-standing beliefs about self, others and relationship which constitute a person's core interpersonal schema will block behaviour in a situation that seems to the observer 'the obvious thing to do' or 'the obvious way out of a dilemma'. Such an option was simply not viable for the person in the original formative context from which the core interpersonal schema is derived. This inhibition has been transferred to the current context and does not appear a possible or safe option for the person concerned. Therapy provides the opportunity for unlocking and releasing such blocked behaviours or of providing genuinely new options to the person/s.

We see the contract in brief-term therapy with couples as devolving on (1) process outcomes and (2) specific behavioural outcomes.

(1) *Process outcomes* are linked to the central dynamic between the partners that can usually be pinpointed as the self-defeating cycle of non-productive interaction they repeatedly become engaged in at stressful times. This cycle is likely to reveal itself at the assessment session, sometimes in response to a question like:
'Will each of you tell me what brings you here?' or 'How does each of you see the problem in your relationship?' In the writers' experience, if partners are given a bit of space to present their own view of the problem, they may very soon disagree and get stuck in the very process that frequently undermines their communication. In this sense, the process is very likely to unfold in front of the therapist giving an immediate and vivid insight into the relationship dynamics. The central 'game', once revealed in the therapeutic setting can then become the focus of the process contract for the brief-term work. Whatever the specific content areas in focus (presenting issues), we have found that the style of (non-) communication that the couple brings to these discussions forms the basis for the 'process contract' in the brief-term therapy. A process contract of this type will involve an identification of the central 'vicious cycle' in the relationship and an agreement to understand, explore and find alternative options for effective communication. This contract will then lead directly to outlining and pinpointing the different stages and elements in the interactive cycle. A review of the core beliefs about self, others and relationship will be an essential part of the therapy. The therapist will also assist the members of the couple to bring to their awareness and find expression for suppressed needs/feelings so that these can then take their rightful and appropriate place in the present relationship.

(2) *Specific behavioural outcomes.* In any brief-term intervention (as in any process of therapy) a good yardstick for assessing effective outcomes is observable behavioural changes. As indicated above, such behavioural changes will be linked and underpinned by intrapsychic (cognitive and affective) shifts in both partners. However acute or deep an insight someone may have gained into a process, the test remains whether the related behaviour change can be made and maintained in the relationship. If new behaviour does not follow insight and understanding, then the therapist may need to reassess the contract and his basic assumptions about the problem arena. Manifest behavioural changes will also serve to give the couple hope in the possibility of change between them even where the intrapsychic change happens more slowly. A person usually

practises a new behaviour many times before she really feels comfortable with it and begins to experience it as truly part of her 'core
self' experience (Stern, 1985).

Specific behavioural contracts are usually directly related to the presenting issues that people bring to the therapy ('We just don't spend much
good time together'; 'I can't remember when last you expressed appreciation for me'; 'We have talked about taking up some activity together,
but we never get that far'; 'We cannot discuss anything without ending
up in a bitter argument and dragging in every resentment from the past';
'You just leave too many of the responsibilities in the home to me'). The
therapist, in accepting and agreeing a behavioural contract, needs to
make clear to the couple that this will involve exploring the reasons why
something is not happening and the process that is blocking their communication. Practising new behaviours in the sessions and homework
assignments are both important in consolidating new options.

In summary, the behavioural contract specifies what the partners want
to do differently or have happen from the other; the process contract
targets the way in which this change is to be implemented, involving
an investigation of those factors which support the status quo and a
proposed change in this underlying frame of reference.

VIABLE AND UNVIABLE CONTRACTS

Contract making is the really crucial part of the therapeutic process
and it is essential to the success of the intervention that the contract
agreed upon is viable and manageable within the time frame. We
favour contracts capable of behavioural validation so that it is clear to
all involved what the gains are and that these can be observed against
changes in behaviour that both partners agree are new, different and
facilitate the communication between them. Desires and hopes such as
'We wish to be happier'; 'We would like to have more fun in our lives
together'; 'We need to find ways of resolving conflict so that things
don't drag on'; 'We want to fight less about sex' may form the basis for
firmer contracting but do not in themselves have the desired specificity. When explored in the assessment session such desires can then
be related to specific behavioural correlates that can be teased out from
the dialogue. Examples: 'We want to express our appreciations as well
as our resentments in clear, straightforward language'; 'We are going

to plan in at least two joint holidays a year to places we both fancy'; 'We want to express our differences, own these and make compromises that suit us both'; 'We want to talk openly about when we do and don't want sex'. The confounding issues in any relationship are usually related to the interactional process that prevents people from clearly expressing or responding to needs. The process outcome focus in the contract will address this level but this is intimately linked to the specific behaviours targeted for change. A focus on specific behavioural outcomes also serves as a barometer of the level of commitment that each partner has to improving the relationship.

Unviable contracts include those that are so vague that it would be impossible to assess whether they have been met or not, e.g. 'We want to be closer to one another'. Such a statement could form the basis for further exploration and could then lead to a specific contract, but in itself it may mean vastly different things to different people. To one partner it may mean more frequent sexual contact, whereas to the other it may mean sharing feelings, hopes and dreams over a cup of tea! Concepts such as 'love', 'fun', 'closeness', 'intimacy', *inter alia*, will have particular idiosyncratic behavioural correlates for different people even though people may share some overall agreement about the meaning of the concepts. Hence our insistence on grounding such discussions in specificity so that people begin to appreciate the differences and recognize the similarities between them. Years of practice have taught us to be cautious about assuming a shared meaning between partners even for frequently used words in their communication.

Unviable contracts may also take the form of unrealistic aspirations and hopes, e.g. 'I want us to be the way we were when we first married before we had children etc . . .', or 'I want us never to disagree' or 'love is never having to say you are sorry'. Some people do indeed have to be educated about what is possible and likely in relationship and what is impossibly idealistic (or pessimistic for that matter). Clearly the internal relationship maps we bring with us into therapy will be coloured by the optimism or pessimism derived from our previous intimate relationships and from earlier childhood experiences of significant others. The popular media also does its fair share to contribute to myths and illusions about couples.

Another type of unviable contract is one that is agreed to because 'I believe I should do . . .' complying with superego demands rather than involving a free informed adult choice based on reality considerations. Many people have internalized a multiplicity of 'shoulds' about marriage and their role in marriage that may be colouring their own feelings and experience of a partner. These prerogatives may need to be articulated and addressed before a viable contract is specified for the sessions. The contract that each partner agrees to needs to be one with which they can identify and take responsibility for fulfilling. We give partners time to reflect on the contract between the assessment session and the first therapy session when it can then be refined and reviewed. A clear contracting process is crucial to the success of brief-term therapy and may sometimes extend beyond the assessment session into the sessions following it. For some couples, the contract may be to arrive at a contract about staying in or leaving their relationship.

Viable contracts will be realistic, manageable within the time frame and the context of the couple's lives and capable of behavioural specificity and validation. Examples: 'We want to share our needs and feelings with each other'; 'We want to develop a way of resolving a conflict between us so that we can both accept the resulting agreement'; 'We wish to develop ways of expressing anger constructively so that we can each have our say and nobody gets physically hurt or walks out on the other'; 'We keep getting stuck in the same old arguments, get upset and nothing ever gets resolved; instead we want to stop this game and be direct and open with each other in our communication'; 'We want to organize our lives in such a way that we can spend time together regularly and develop some joint interests beyond the family', 'We want to express our care for one another in ways that really meet the need of the other'. Each of these contracts will require working towards both process and specific behavioural goals.

THE RELATIONSHIP BETWEEN THE CONTRACT AND THE THERAPEUTIC AIMS AND GOALS

The contract as agreed upon will invariably relate to one or more of the areas covered by the assessment. Some contracts will be focused on the area of intimacy; others on the problem-solving arena; others more particularly on how caring is defined and how demonstrated between partners. Some people may be really stuck at the point of not understanding or appreciating each other's perspective on relationship or the priorities of the other and will make a contract to explore the value base of the relationship. In subsequent chapters we will be looking at these different problem areas in some detail and suggesting specific interventions that relate to the different relationship dimensions.

The over-arching challenge for the therapist in every case will contain two questions in common:

• What is preventing these two people from resolving this problem?
• What is the learning that they each need to do in order to move forward?

This questioning will lead directly to an appreciation of the intersubjective communication issue that leads two people to get stuck in a particular way in the process of problem resolution. This does not mean pushing everyone towards a similar model of relationship; it means identifying why these two unique human beings cannot come to a mutual understanding that promotes their relationship or supports an agreement that they do not wish to pursue.

THE CONTRACTUAL PROCESS IN RELATIONSHIPS

We have been writing here of the importance of an initial contract or agreed-upon goal in brief-term therapy to ensure the success of the intervention. However, we wish to emphasize too our belief in the significant role that the contractual *process* can play in all human relationships. The initial contracting will serve as a model for the couple of how to reach an agreement in other instances and give them a learning experience of the role that contracting could play in their ongoing relationship. The contractual process is based upon a respect for the other and a belief that each person is able to negotiate in a reasonable and satisfactory manner about important issues in their lives. When we 'contract' in this way with another, we are respecting the other's right to say 'no', to agree or disagree with us, and we are expressing our trust in the capacity of the other to meet us half-way in the process. In this sense, contracting is underpinned by a value of mutual respect and a willingness to share, to cooperate and to agree satisfactory compromises in order to promote relationship goals. Each person states clearly and unequivocally what they will and will not do, and that agreement is kept by the partners unless renegotiated or reformulated.

A contractual approach in relationship also means that I do not take for granted that the other will like what I like or will do what I want, but carefully check out their position before making assumptions about issues. Careful checking out before presuming on another's wishes or desires may initially seem pedantic and artificial. Some have objected that such a process may 'inhibit spontaneity' and lead to emotional restraint in a relationship. We acknowledge such objections and would not wish for people to inhibit spontaneous expressions of affection. However, it is useful, particularly in areas known to involve conflict or differing priorities, to use the process of contracting to agree goals and plans of action. As novel ways of behaving and relating become more habitual, they will also lose the constraint and self-conscious intention that originally accompanies the practice of new options. As a change of behaviour evokes more rewarding responses, this new 'evidence' will feed back into the core interpersonal schema gradually altering a person's belief system and impacting on their experience of self. In this way people gradually build up new and different senses of self that may fit better with their basic organismic functioning and bring them closer to the kind of satisfaction they desire in their intimate relationships.

6

WORKING THROUGH THE ISSUE OF COMPATIBILITY OF VALUE SYSTEMS AND FRAMES OF REFERENCE

COMPATIBILITY AND INCOMPATIBILITY OF VALUES AND BELIEF SYSTEMS

Compatibility in basic values and assumptions forms the bedrock of a relationship, since values govern people's priorities and will influence all the choices they make, whether large or small. Our beliefs are incorporated in the cognitive schemata that we have developed over the years. These are often so embedded in our thinking that we are not consciously aware of the assumptions that govern our choices until someone expresses surprise at one of our preferences. (Why do we always have to go to the pub to relax? Why not invite people home or meet them in a restaurant?) Frames of reference are influenced and contributed to by each person's personal and historical background which shapes an individual's values. Beliefs are often implicit rather than explicitly stated, so that a person may accept as 'reality', what is actually an interpretation of experience based on beliefs. It is easy to come to believe that 'this is the way things are' because they have always been that way in our families and cultures of origin. In this sense 'things are what they seem to us' and we may defend as 'the truth' what is only one interpretation of a situation or one way of doing things.

The main source of conflict in certain relationships revolves around such differences in priorities which are linked with clashes in basic values. If each party is convinced that their own values are the 'right' and only ones, this can result in endless disputes about whose point of view is correct. The therapist will need to resist taking sides in these disputes, although the tendency to be drawn in is some-times difficult to resist. Even when the therapist is clearly not sup-porting one or the other, one party may still define the therapist as 'ganging up against me' or 'entirely on my side'. The competition about who is 'right' may be a defence against a deep-seated insec-urity about acceptability as a person. In such disputes both partners are defending themselves against the feeling that there is something 'wrong with me'. So the argument becomes a survival level issue about whose needs for love and approval will be met in the relation-ship. In such competitive systems, the underlying assumption is that only one person's needs are valid and if one wins it must mean that the other loses. The challenge to the therapist is to stay out of the game of 'Courtroom' by not setting himself up as the judge while at the same time stressing that the issue is about understanding the other and not about ruling on the rights and wrongs of people's world views.

A helpful intervention for the therapist to make if he is focusing on a contract related to discrepancies in defining roles and tasks in a rela-tionship is to ask the following questions that may reveal underlying assumptions about these issues. This exercise can be particularly illuminating if people are separated by issues of class, culture, race or religion.

● What do you expect of yourself in this relationship/marriage?
● What do you expect of your partner in this relationship/marriage?
● What are your expectations and beliefs about the nature of relation-ship/marriage?

These questions open up the implicit level of beliefs that subtly deter-mine the process between the two people and may underpin many of the conflicts that result in arguments about priorities. They also touch on the meaning of the relationship to the partners and will reveal cultural and class differences. For example, the place of romantic love in relationships may vary greatly, depending on people's backgrounds and heritages. Class differences will influence many details in people's lives from their choice of food to their expectations of their children, themselves and even of life's possibilities.

CULTURE SHAPES OUR FRAMES OF REFERENCE

The importance of early experience on subsequent adult development and functioning is axiomatic in psychological theories. Our families of origin are central in determining many of our attitudes and beliefs particularly those in regard to relationships. Our roles, both conscious and unconscious, our values, ethics, beliefs and behaviours arise in our families. Particularly in collectivist cultures, family values are currently given more importance than in western ones, where many family structures are breaking down and lip service only is paid by media and politicians to family values. This discrepancy between what is spoken of as important and what is actually happening creates a challenge for people who are thrown back on their own individual resources or may imbibe their values from adolescent sub-cultures, tight religious affiliations and in extreme cases from cults.

Many people are unaware of the powerful impact of their deeply embedded cultural assumptions about roles, expectations and task definitions in intimate relationships. Culture is one of several significant factors that contribute to our ways of framing and understanding interpersonal situations. Class, religion, race, education, gender, socio-economic status and our own unique and idiosyncratic family constellation will likewise shape our assumptions of ourselves and others in relationship. Tradition prescribes male and female roles, but in this climate of rapid change in sex role definitions, considerable anxiety is generated by the challenge to people to find their own position which may be very different from the role adopted by the same-sex parent in the previous generation. In western cultures, the dominant role of men as the breadwinners and protectors, and women as the homemakers and nurturers is rapidly shifting as women move into the workplace. This change impacts significantly on the task of the couples therapist. Said to the therapist by a partner in a couple who had been married for twenty years and were readdressing the balance between dependence and independence when the wife decided to retrain and return to the job market: 'You simply don't understand; she's just not the girl that I married any more . . .'.

Part of the impact of the changing roles of men and women has resulted in more men presenting for therapy with the problem that their wives have suddenly and wholly unexpectedly (for the man) decided to leave the relationship after many years because of a deep-seated and embedded dissatisfaction with the traditional role ascribed to her and in a desire for independence. Similarly many women have moved out of a longstanding marriage into a relationship with a woman, disillusioned with the possibility of intimacy or closeness with a man and ready to explore and own a different dimension of relatedness. These are some of the challenges that currently present to the couples therapist, who is often faced with the task of assisting the couple to negotiate a creative separation and to deal with the unchartered territory of the new relationship.

One of the most widely spread ways in which cultural difference has been conceptualized is along what has been described as the individual–collectivist divide. The individualistic culture typified by western post-industrialism is one in which the emphasis is on the individual, an individual whose identity is defined in terms of free choices. In contrast, collectivist cultures are those in which the tightly knit family and social groups are central in defining identity, values, attitudes and behaviours.

A pertinent example of the formation of relationships would be to consider how differently love and love connections are viewed from these two perspectives. In collectivist cultures, not only does love not have a legitimate place in the formation of marriage, but free choice of a partner is regarded as too fragile to be left to individual choice. Thus from its inception a partnership formed across these two views, where the western one by way of contrast regards love as the most significant component, is fraught with difficulty and pressures. There is little evidence, in fact, that one style of partner selection is necessarily better than another. This conflict however may frame and obscure other areas of difficulty such as conflicts arising from different familial and cultural expectations.

With the mass movements of people across cultures, both within and between countries, nationalities, classes and religions, relationships and partnerships across these divides are increasingly likely to occur. The couples therapist is more frequently facing the challenge of helping partners in a cross-cultural or interracial partnership. Furthermore children of migrant and immigrant groups are likely to become more westernized in countries like the UK or the USA. In the face of conflicting value systems the tendency is to adopt western values because western, individualistic life styles seem to offer young people a way of obtaining liberation from families and their perceived constraints.

However, this process can bring a powerful clash of value systems in its wake, both intrapsychically and interpersonally.

The differences in individual and cultural experience have much relevance for the brief-term intervention described, since it is both the broad cultural differences as well as the idiosyncratic configurations found in couples that could reveal widely different notions, ideas, expectations, hopes and fears about the other. These psychological aspects are both conscious and in awareness as well as out of awareness but nonetheless influencing behaviour patterns and styles of relating. From our perspective then, people's frames of reference and their understanding of the differences between them are crucial to this work, since they have a broad and far-reaching impact on the thoughts, feelings and behaviours that couples have with regard to many issues.

DIFFERENCES ARISING FROM RELIGION, EDUCATION AND CLASS

When marriage partners have different religious affiliations, the clash in their frames of reference can often lead to extremes of stress and tension, especially if either or both cherish a deep-seated conviction that his/her religion is the 'true' one. However tolerant people may appear on the surface, religious beliefs run deep and a difference of religions calls for a toleration of diversity and an acceptance of the other person's right to adhere to their own religious rites. Religious beliefs also affect many daily issues that impact on the relationship, attitudes to food, to spare time, to sex and to the raising of children. It is therefore crucial that the differences in belief structures be 'heard', accepted and respected if the relationship is to flourish.

In the case of Arthur and Colleen's marriage, their religious differences were an issue from the start. Colleen, as a devout Catholic, wished to get married in the Catholic church. To Arthur who had been brought up as an Anglican and attended an Anglican boarding school, this desire seemed like a betrayal and an assault on all he held dear in terms of church, hearth and home. He suggested that they compromise by getting married in both churches, but again Colleen's beliefs prohibited this arrangement. Finally Arthur reluctantly agreed to get married in the Roman Catholic church, although he remained unhappy at what he perceived as the inflexibility manifested by Colleen, her family

and the local priest in this matter. Their marriage was marked by fairly
regular disagreements on issues such as contraception, the religion of
the children and Colleen's desire for Arthur to consider converting to
her faith. In another instance, Sharita, who was Hindu married Hussein, who was a Muslim. Sharita came from a westernized family who
had been living in England for many years, and in which a large
degree of independence was accorded all the children in the family.
Hussein had only recently arrived in the country when the two got
married. Sharita found the role expectations on her as a woman difficult to accommodate, as well as the pressure to convert to Islam. A
particular problem in this marriage arose from the unacceptability of
Sharita to the wider Muslim community. In another instance, when
Jane married Hymie, she converted to Judaism from Presbyterianism.
They were aided by a brief intervention to adjust to their respective
perceptions of what this would mean in terms of issues like 'keeping
kosher', the religious education of their children and related issues.

The class divide in Britain can also affect relationships where partners
come from different strata in society. For example in a marriage where
James was from an upper class British family and Shirley from a working class background, James was concerned in the presence of his
extended family that Shirley would 'let him down' by her accent, her
preference for certain types of food and her 'ignorance about the
theatre'. His family in turn would make fun of her openly or subtly
and at times even snub her if they were at a large social gathering.
Shirley, who was ready to believe in her inferiority from years of
hearing that she was 'second best', struggled with this process which
was seriously alienating her from James at the time they consulted a
therapist. Education can also contribute to rifts in relationship where
one partner is threatened or envious of the educational achievements
of the other – which, of course, is not automatically the case. In one
instance, Mary, who was from a working class Irish family living on a
council estate, had been given a private education by her parents in
their desire to 'uplift the family'. Mary subsequently married a man
from Scotland who was from a working class background himself who
prided themselves on their status: 'We've done fine and there's no
need for all that private school stuff!' When Mary insisted on going to
University and obtaining her MA degree, the tensions in her marriage
led her to seek help. Where couples are also dealing with intercultural
and interracial differences, the challenge to deal with the diversity
between them creatively becomes that much greater.

SAME SEX COUPLES: ISSUES THAT HOMOSEXUAL MEN BRING TO THERAPY

Gay male couples will share many relationship issues with all other couples and will be assessed along similar dimensions. It is important to keep in mind, however, that they form part of an oppressed and often despised minority, so that some of the things that heterosexual couples would take for granted constitute matters of anxiety and conscious choice. (Do we let the neighbours in our new neighbourhood know that we are a couple or do we keep that aspect of our lives hidden?) In consultation with colleagues who are experienced in working with gay men, from our own practice with this group and from the literature, we have summarized a few of the problems that may currently particularly characterize gay male couples.

How do you deal with monogamy in gay society where sex is very overt and easily available? Partners struggle with the issue of monogamy especially when the prevailing culture at gathering points very obviously does not support this choice. They may wish to socialize but the expectation and opportunity will constantly be before them to engage in casual sex or embark on another concurrent sexual encounter. Another issue often brought to therapy is that of role expectations and the division of tasks in the relationship. There are no easily accessible role models for gay male couples. Society scripts men to be strong, assume authority and leadership in close relationships. If both partners have received similar gender role scripting, then a new and creative renegotiation of roles will need to take place. A frequent challenge for couples in this position is to find expression for feelings of tenderness and love, which are often prohibited in men by cultural norms. 'The fact of having an intimate sexual relationship with a person of the same sex does not always liberate a gay couple from all the other aspects of a gender-polarized culture' (Singer in Wheeler and Backman, 1994). In the course of brief therapy with Brewster and Jack, the therapist asked each of them what expectations of 'being a man' they had internalized as children. In both cases the role model was very conventional and required them to be breadwinners, whilst any 'feminine' jobs involving home-making were allotted to women. Jack and Brewster acknowledged that each secretly believed the other should take on the tasks of home-making. Once they talked about this openly, they were able to agree a division of labour that resulted in Brewster uncovering an interest in flower-arranging and Jack a passionate interest in cooking.

Another presenting problem is that of the older man who joins with a much younger man; several years on in the relationship the dependent younger man may want more freedom and space, while the older man wishes to retain the original dependent symbiotic relationship. Yet another common theme is the loss of interest in sex with a partner after one or two years and a desire on the part of this person for sexual activities with others outside of the core relationship. The other partner may be left desiring a continuance of the original sexual contact in the partnership. A colleague views this as the operation of the psychological split between love and sex (love without sex or sex without love being the equations). This issue may widen the emotional gulf between the partners if not openly addressed. Many couples continue to live together as companions for years, each having separate sexual relationships outside of the partnership. Such agreements may work well for all the people concerned. However, we have known problems to arise if one of the people involved develops AIDS; then the question becomes who looks after and takes care of the person who is ill.

Finally there is the question of dealing with HIV and AIDS. If one partner is HIV positive and the other is not, this can lead to a number of psychological complexities in the relationship. The affected partner may start resenting the fact that the other is free of the virus and has plenty of energy for activities outside the home, whilst the partner with AIDS finds his activities progressively more circumscribed. In some cases, the unaffected partner may cherish a romantic notion that he should become infected so that he is HIV positive as well and can share in this way the other's experience, so that they can die together. This problem may well be related to the concept of 'survivor guilt' (Lifton, 1993) which is often associated with the survivors of tragedy and forms a familiar component of post-traumatic stress disorders. Where one partner dies of AIDS and the other starts a new relationship, the partner who joins him may find that he is living with the ongoing 'presence' of an idealized dead partner. This process can place a great strain on the developing relationship.

These constitute a few of the presenting issues that brief-term therapists may face in dealing with gay male couples. Our intention cannot hope to be comprehensive, but to give a representative sample of current presenting issues in this population.

SAME-SEX COUPLES: ISSUES THAT LESBIAN WOMEN BRING TO THERAPY

Lesbian women will also present with issues along the relationship dimensions outlined in our chapter on assessment. Again it is crucial to remember that this group is subjected to societal oppression which provides an added complication to the therapy process. A lesbian partnership does not have automatic legal or social validity and many of the issues the partners face in relationship may be related to aspects of this lack of social and legal status. Because of immigration laws partners who are resident in different countries may find that they are separated and do not have the option of marriage and entry into one another's countries. They are then forced to conduct a 'distance' relationship with its attendant stresses and strains. In the course of therapy Genevieve who lived in Canada and Yvonne who lived in England faced the question of how to manage a relationship that would inevitably result in their seeing one another for only limited periods of time, interspersed with separations. The therapist helped them to express the grief associated with their life situation and then to make realistic contracts about issues like fidelity, monogamy and shared assets.

Couples will all face the question of whether they choose to 'come out' or not. The ease with which women can 'come out' as lesbians is mediated by class, education, geography, age, income and their work setting. In some professions, such as social work, teaching and nursing, it has often appeared easier for women to be open about their sexual orientation, because of the presence of many others in a similar position. However, the effect of recent legislation has been to inhibit this process. Many couples prefer to keep their relationship hidden: 'As long as we are quiet about it, nobody minds. If we come out, then people will be forced to take a disapproving stand'. Whatever the therapist's own stance on issues such as these, she needs to bracket these and be sensitive to the partners' decisions about their life-style.

Because of the censure that is often present in relation to lesbian couples and because of the oppression referred to above, lesbian couples show an inclination to enter into and remain in symbiotic relationships. 'Given that lesbian couples are denied legal status in this culture, confluence can serve as a strategy to cope with heterosexism by providing a sense of relationship stability' (F. Curtis in Wheeler and Backman, 1994). Such couples bring to therapy the issue of dealing with individual needs and differences, as they begin to experience the constraints imposed by the initial symbiosis.

There are not many role models for life together as a lesbian couple. Some couples will take on the heterosexual nuclear model of marriage and then discover that this does not meet their needs. Jasmin and Pat brought to therapy the issue of whether to share a common home. Jasmin, who was Asian, reported that there was no acceptance in her culture for her lesbianism and that as a result of it she would be cast out of the extended family and probably denied further contact with family members. She did not feel ready or able to face such drastic consequences of her choice of partner, so she wished for her and Pat to live separately but spend most of their time together. Pat, in her turn, felt 'rejected' by this suggestion, had become jealous of Jasmin's family and did not see how Jasmin could make such a suggestion if their relationship was a priority for her. Jasmin had to contend in addition with the oppression that resulted from being a black woman in a society where she was often subtly or overtly open to discrimination.

Lesbian couples who choose to have children are faced with the complexities of a family structure that does not fit the nuclear family structure and expectations. The partners may come for help in dealing with issues children raise especially once they go to school and need to negotiate a predominantly heterosexual world. Where one partner has children from a heterosexual marriage relationship, she may find that if she reveals that she has a new lesbian partner she is very unlikely to get custody of her children. If one partner chooses to have a child and the other does not, the other partner may find the role of unacknowledged step-parent extremely taxing.

Women who choose a lesbian life-style in mid-life may suddenly come up against prejudice for the first time in their lives or find that they have to deal with their own internalized homophobia. In one case dealt with by one of the writers, Minnie was so horrified to realize her lesbian tendencies that she decided that only a sex-change operation could remedy the situation. As a man who felt attracted to a woman she would not then have to face her own internal censure – concerned with severe cultural and religious prohibitions of same-sex love. On exploration, Minnie revealed that she experienced herself very much as a woman and that her identity had always been as 'feminine', but her strong religious convictions labelled her as a 'sinner' for being attracted sexually to another woman. The only solution she could see to the problem was to change her sex so that she could fit within accepted parameters. Such severe homophobia required a multi-faceted intervention, of which two periods of brief couples therapy formed the initial and also the final stages.

We have given here a sample of the problems currently brought to couples therapy by lesbian couples. These examples are drawn from our own experience and that of some of our professional colleagues who work in the same field.

ISSUES BROUGHT TO THERAPY BY MIXED RACE COUPLES AND BY COUPLES OF DUAL DESCENT (INTERCULTURAL AND INTERRACIAL PARTNERSHIPS)

Issues brought to therapy by couples of dual descent often involve different interpretations of behaviour, misunderstanding of different cultural roles, divergent attitudes to child-rearing, money and spending. There is sometimes a confusion about what is cultural, what is racial and what is personal, leading to the question: 'When do I need to compromise because this is a cultural norm that is important to my partner, and when am I dealing with some personal idiosyncrasy of behaviour that is individual to this person?' In some cultures a family conference will come to decisions that intimately impact upon the couple; whereas in other cultures such decisions are made by the individuals. In the case of the family conference the partner of a 'different' race may even be excluded from the family conference and then be expected to abide by decisions in which he/she had no share at all. Such a different attitude to decision-making can lead to much stress and misunderstanding.

For example a particular couple presented for therapy with the following intercultural and interracial issue. Gladys comes from an African culture where the men are regarded as 'proper' men if they watch sport, drink beer, fix things around the house, work on their cars and make the family decisions. Aaron was raised by a single parent. His mother came from an intellectual musical family. Being her only child, he was actively discouraged by her from taking part in sport. He had violin lessons and learnt tap dancing as a child. Gladys does not appreciate his love of classical music and was particularly disconcerted on holiday when he could not change a wheel on their car. Her difficulty is compounded by knowing her family's judgements on her choice of a 'softie' as a partner. She views Aaron's tendency to consult her on all matters as weakness on his part and has difficulty in accepting the importance he places on mutuality in decision-making. He in turn has little sympathy for the cultural norms that Gladys has grown up to value and expect. Building a respect for difference was the initial focus of the therapy.

The question of who is to take the more dominant role in a relationship is very much influenced by culture and family background. In the case of Jasper who was from Jamaica and married Jennifer who is English, dominance was an ongoing relationship issue. Jasper worked as an unqualified chef who was well-respected in his place of work. Jennifer had recently completed her first degree and wished to continue to obtain a higher degree. This process put a strain on their relationship since Jasper felt that he would 'no longer be good enough for her' and that he would 'not be respected in his own family'. Jennifer reacted strongly to the constraints and consequently the tensions in their relationship steadily increased. It was at this point that they sought help.

Anjeli and Angus presented for therapy because they were feeling alienated from one another. Their challenge in a relationship that requires each of them to respect the race and culture of the other was how to preserve a sense of self-identity whilst also making allowances for the cultural and racial differences. Intellectually they accept the differences between them, but emotionally certain behaviours provoke disapproval. For example, Angus realizes that eating with one's hands is part of Anjeli's Asian tradition, but the problem arises about the way she does this in that he considers that she is 'messy'. This embarrasses him particularly when his family come to visit. Coming from a Scottish tradition that values 'good manners', they were nothing short of horrified by Anjeli's traditions. This is only one example of the type of stress that was impinging on their relationship.

BELIEFS AND ASSUMPTIONS ABOUT THE NATURE OF CHANGE

Deeply embedded in people's frames of reference are assumptions about the desirability and the possibility of change and the process by which change occurs. If change is perceived to threaten a person's world view and to be disruptive of cultural or religious practices, such a person will find the process of coming to couples therapy profoundly disturbing. The couples therapist is well advised to check on how each partner believes that change will take place in the relationship and in the context of the therapy, since sometimes people believe that simply attending the sessions will magically produce the desired results (which is usually that the other party will adopt my frame of reference). You may also come up against the person who does not believe that change is possible and has only come along to placate the other or to be seen to be willing to try. The therapist will educate people about the process of working at change by making specific contracts for new behaviours. The fact that relationships may need to be worked at and require ongoing care in order to thrive comes as a surprise to those people who hold on to a fairytale notion of meeting Mr/Ms Right with whom magically all is imagined to run smoothly ever after. In addition, the therapist will encourage the partners to use the therapy time to examine dearly held beliefs and to express underlying feelings that may relate to the concept of change. ('If I change, I'm afraid you won't love me anymore'.)

INTERVENING IN THE COUPLE'S BELIEF SYSTEMS

A useful and necessary approach in the sessions is to address each individual's belief system, in relation to the central dynamics and the main areas of conflict. The beliefs usually cluster around a system of beliefs about self, others and the quality of life. This belief system is associated with concomitant behaviours, feelings, fantasies and memories (Erskine and Zalcman, 1979). This approach explores how each individual's way of organizing and structuring their experience interlocks with and triggers aspects of the other partner's in such a way that it will evoke or reinforce aspects of their scripts. Working with interlocking scripts highlights how partners select each other for conscious and unconscious reasons. The positive side of unconscious mate selection is connected to the hope that the other will free them from their past and from the script. The unconscious aspect is how people inevitably choose partners who reinforce or repeat unhappy patterns from the past. Looking at the repeating self-defeating and unproductive styles of relating and functioning in terms of interlocking scripts is another way of describing the repetition compulsion. 'Each relationship can be viewed as having its own inherent problems, many of which arise from the very forces that attracted the individuals to each other in the first place.' (Wile, 1981, p. 204).

In counselling or therapy, it is possible to enter this script system through beliefs, feelings or behaviour and then explore and understand how it was constructed as a way of trying to cope with early unmet needs. In couple's work instead of using the therapeutic relationship or the fantasy of fulfilment in the past, the counsellor can direct the energy to the other partner. This work not only leads to insight and understanding by each partner of their own and their partner's scripts, but also creates the opportunity for the needs to be understood and accepted within the framework of the relationship. Moving and freeing emotional work occurs within this frame and creates change possibilities both intrapsychically and interpersonally. Intervening in the couple's system allows for the change process to continue and be powerfully reinforced outside therapeutic sessions. Once the constrictions and restraints of the outdated frame of reference and the way the repeating patterns occur, reinforcing each other, have been understood, it is really difficult to go back to the unproductive, sterile arguments. The understanding of the way the other reinforces and takes a place in the system leads to the unlocking of those repeating cycles and change so that different, more creative options become possible. 'It is a well-known psychoanalytic principle that people form relationships to solve certain lifelong problems.' (Wile, 1981, p. 204).

This therapeutic exploration allows people to examine their belief structures and frames of reference to see whether they still hold up in the here and now and in the context of the present relationship. A simple format for analysing such interlocking patterns is supplied in Figure 1 in Chapter 3. This can used by the therapist to inform his interventions or it can be used as an intervention of itself when the therapist draws it up together with the partners who supply the relevant information. Once the 'vicious cycle' in the communication has been depicted in this way, therapist and clients alike can discover alternative strategies to this process.

Another important issue to be addressed by the therapist is the place or position the particular therapist may be invited to assume in the couple's system. This is another way of keeping in mind the transference and counter-transference issues that inevitably occur in any therapeutic contacts. That transference occurs is inevitable, how one chooses to use it or work with it depends on the frame, goals and context. In brief work in general the transferential issues, although held in mind, would not be emphasized. A good question for the therapist to reflect upon is: 'What role does this couple unconsciously desire me to adopt in relating to them?' For example, the therapist may be cast in the role of the 'wise elder' in the community who is appealed to for advice and guidance; or the 'fairy godmother' who will magically make everything right again; or the therapist may be seen as the critical arbiter of society's values who will not brook any divergence from them. It is crucial for the therapist to identify and to name this embedded expectation so that she does not slip into this role unconsciously but negotiates realistic expectations of her proposed part in the brief-term therapy.

EXERCISES AND POSSIBLE HOMEWORK ASSIGNMENTS RELATED TO VALUES AND BELIEFS

We will describe a few representative exercises that relate to values and belief systems, which can, at appropriate times, either be used within the session or set as 'homework' for those couples for whom they are relevant.

Choosing or Designing a House

In this exercise partners are instructed to choose or design a house that will have a certain number of rooms (to be specified at the outset and reflect the cultural norm). They are given specifications for the overall floor space of the house and then asked to decide on both the relative size and the use that will be put to the different rooms in their house. They are asked to discuss and negotiate with each other until they come to an agreement about how the space is to be used. They are also asked to note what differences in priorities arise in these discussions. This exercise has a light-hearted aspect to it, but when seriously undertaken as a task has revealed interesting discrepancies in priorities sometimes related to deep-seated differences in life choices. ('Of course, I need an office at home!'; 'We need to keep a room ready for my mother's visits.')

Sharing Shoulds or Assumptions

We are indebted for the inspiration in this exercise to Stevens (1971) whose book *'Awareness'* is an invaluable resource for the couples or group therapist. In this exercise, the couple is asked to experiment with completing the following sentence as often as possible within an agreed period of time (e.g. five minutes), 'In our relationship, I assume that you . . .'. They can then switch for a further five minutes to completing the sentence: 'In this relationship, I assume that I . . .'. An alternative version is for each person to write down as many of the 'shoulds' as they are able to access from their internalized store (derived from their families and cultures of origin) and then to evaluate the extent to which these still exert an influence on their lives. They can then re-evaluate these 'shoulds' in the light of present realities and decide how these may be changed or updated to suit their current needs and life situation.

Listing and Grading Values (Priorities) in Order of Importance to the Individual

In this task the partners are asked to list their priorities, initially in any order, and then to grade these in order of importance to them. They can then compare theirs with their partner's. This can lead to fruitful discussion and re-evaluation of joint endeavours.

We Will Give a Final Exercise to Explore Views on the Process of Change

This is particularly recommended where people project the responsibility for change onto others and expect change to happen to them from the outside. Partners are asked to answer the following questions: What was your mother's attitude to change? What was your father's attitude to change? What is your attitude to change? The answers to these simple questions often reveal family beliefs about how change happens, how people handle it when it does and generally about the desirability or otherwise of change. Beliefs about the possibility or desirability of change may profoundly affect people's attitudes to therapy and the therapist.

7

WORKING THROUGH THE AREAS OF EFFECTIVE PROBLEM-SOLVING AND CONFLICT RESOLUTION

In this chapter we cover the areas of problem-solving, conflict resolution and fair fighting in relationship. This dimension involves the capacity for clear, straight communication and the refinement of techniques and strategies for problem-resolution. Where this is a deficit in relationships, couples often get tangled in long arguments and emotional exchanges that may have little relevance to the issue originally under consideration. We have outlined some of the issues, described the role of the therapist in creating a safe space for experimentation and have made some suggestions regarding possible interventions into the couple system. We have added relevant exercises and homework assignments at the end of the discussion section.

THE ROLE OF THE EMOTIONS IN PROBLEM-SOLVING

The resolution of problems requires an integration of affect, cognition and behaviour. A person needs to assess the external situation accurately, check their own feelings and needs in relation to the imminent decision or action and implement appropriate behaviour. Gathering the relevant information involves all these three areas. The external check on the environment yields information in the field that relates to the issue. The internal organismic check yields information about the person's feelings and needs relating to the problem to be solved. These two areas are combined to yield the information necessary for effective action. If one is ignored at the cost of the other, the solution arrived at and acted upon will be based on biased and slanted information. If a person is too internally bound up, he may not attend sufficiently to reality factors in the external environment or take cognizance of the needs of others. If a person is too externally focused, she may disregard or minimize her own needs and act in a way that 'solves' the problem but at a cost to her own wellbeing.

Many people believe that they cannot think and feel at the same time, a belief that can interfere with effective problem-solving. Some people may define themselves as 'thinkers' and 'good at problem-solving', although their solutions frequently minimize their own needs and feelings. In this way, they end up frustrated, believing that they are 'always left carrying the can' or 'being strong when everyone else around them collapses'. Such people need to heighten their awareness of their own emotional needs and integrate these into their effective planning strategies. They may appear very effective at getting things done, but this can be at considerable personal cost. These people were often the 'little parents' in their families of origin where they were required to take adult responsibility before their time. When they enter relationships as adults, they very readily assume the problem-solving role and take over that function, only to realize later that their own needs have become submerged in this process. It is almost as if what they do well, they do too well for their own (or finally the other's) good. Such a ready assumption of responsibility as the prime problem solver may keep the other partner in a dependent role where that person's capacity to think and sort out difficulties is neither honoured nor given the scope for development. Such an unequal partnership may present for help when the dependent partner starts differentiating, or when the 'problem-solver' begins to realize the extent to which he has ignored his own tender feelings and dependency needs. He has deprived both himself and his partner of the intimate contact that is the basis of relationship.

Other people may define themselves as 'emotional and intuitive', and not primarily consider themselves as thinkers. Valuing their feelings highly, they often act impulsively and 'spontaneously' without considering the impact of their behaviour on others or evaluating the consequences of their actions for themselves. They have usually been regarded as the 'sensitive, intuitive' child in the family of origin, whose logical thinking capacities were not encouraged or valued. Their capacity to feel into the heart of a matter may lead them to take action before they have done a comprehensive environmental check. They can end up feeling hurt: 'You don't appreciate my feelings'; 'I put so much of myself into our relationship, and all I get is an irritable response'. Assessing the impact of their behaviour on others and also a careful evaluation of the likely consequences of their actions for themselves is the learning they need to acquire.

Both these styles of relating to problems result in unbalanced solutions. The challenge in both cases is similar – to integrate and balance thinking and feeling so that personal needs are taken into account in the consequent choice of action. The consequences of a decision need to be carefully evaluated for all concerned parties. It is not unusual for partners with these two differing relationship styles to come together and struggle with accommodating to each other's very different styles of relating to relevant information. At its best this provides each of them with the opportunity to learn from the other what is missing in their own style; at its worst it may lead to recurrent fights and recriminations about a lack of understanding on the part of the other.

In working through the areas of effective problem-solving and conflict resolution, it is essential to mobilize people's capacity to think effectively, with reference both to internal information concerning their needs and also with reference to the accurate assessment of external realities. The areas that people need to think about are often emotionally laden and difficult to address. Strong emotions can initially interfere with one's capacity to solve problems. The counselling situation provides the opportunity for the expression of such emotions in a protected space and then offers the possibility for intellectual integration and reflection. This process of integration is an essential prerequisite to effective action. Thus, central to the therapist's role is the creation of a safe and protected place for the exploration and expression of emotional needs.

CREATING SAFETY AND CONTAINMENT

The sense of safety is created in the first place by establishing firm boundaries. Boundaries are set in place around the counselling, which protects it from intrusion from the outside world, as well as bound-aries within the space so that partners are protected from physical and verbal abuse which will cause further damage to themselves or the relationship. Establishing firm boundaries involves specific contracts about number, length and frequency of sessions. The partners are also asked to make an agreement not to verbally abuse or physically damage each other, the therapist or the therapeutic space. Verbal abuse often takes the form of blaming, humiliating or labelling the other in an offensive and degrading manner. The focused therapeutic goals of brief-term therapy, which are articulated in the therapeutic contracts, also serve to provide a boundary around the work that is being under-taken by the couple and the therapist.

Consciously or unconsciously couples will save some of their major conflicts for the sessions. They may often begin to discuss an issue on their way to therapy or quarrel slightly before a session so that they can show the therapist 'how bad it is' or 'have the fight' in the thera-pist's presence. In many cases, they may sense the need for a safe and contained fight, being too frightened of the possibility of uncontrolled aggression: 'I really need to discuss this urgently, but I was afraid that we would get into the usual hopeless wrangle on our own so I saved it for the session'. We have already referred to some couples' desire for a referee or judge. The pressure on the therapist to adopt this role is great, yet it is crucial for him/her to remain neutral even though at times it is necessary to intervene on behalf of one of the protagonists. When the therapist does this, a discussion of the reasons motivating this intervention may help to restore a sense of balance in the therapy. The therapist is sometimes a mediator in the sense of ensuring that partners are listening to one another. Because the therapist is the prim-ary guardian of the therapeutic contract, she will refer back to the contract regularly in an effort to ensure that the focus of the therapy is not lost. As a mediator, the therapist's task is to maintain her empathy for both partners in order to keep a safe boundary around the therapy.

In the case of the potential for an uncontrolled aggressive outburst, the therapist will intervene and contain this by addressing the underlying threat or fear that fuels these attacks. Where this can be worked with, the freeing of energy may enable the partners to have cleaner fights in the future. At the same time, the therapist can bring them to a clearer understanding of the meaning and effect of the uncontained aggres-sion and also the unresolved and painful issues that give rise to this level of anger. The origins of rage and primitive feelings frequently lie in people's developmental histories and are related to situations and experiences that feel like injuries to the sense of self, especially where it feels as if real or psychological survival is at stake. Our earlier references to shame-based systems is also relevant here. If certain feelings and needs have been associated with humiliation and shame in earlier years, then the person is likely to react violently, angrily and protectively when such hidden emotions are activated. This is frequently the basis of much desperate fighting in relationships. Therapy offers the opportunity for the surfacing of these feelings and needs – often feelings of vulnerability or expressions of tenderness, fear, sadness or love.

As much as it is necessary to provide safety and containment for strong negative feelings, such as hate and envy, so too paradoxically there are times when people fear the strong expression of love and care, even when they believe they long for such experiences. Out of this anxiety, they will attack expressions of closeness or try to avoid contact by becoming 'gamey' and aggressive. The need to attack these feelings is related to the fear of the pain that arises as the memories of unmet childhood needs and the yearning for closeness are unlocked by the evocation of the longed-for contact. The safety of therapy provides a context where such tender emotions can gradually surface without fear of humiliation so that the associated needs for closeness and contact can be met in the partnership.

Clearly then it is not only important for the therapist to avoid triangulation and slipping into the position of role or judge, it is also necessary for the therapist to be able to manage and contain the expression of strong emotions. This would include the ability to manage their own strong feelings, as well as having worked through their own internal position in relation to the management and expression of aggression, fear, sadness and love. If the therapist himself experiences a shame-bind associated with the expression of any of the basic emotions, this is likely to be triggered by the clients and he may end up colluding with their suppression of this emotion.

It is likewise necessary to have the self awareness and insight as a therapist as to how he/she may use, manipulate or control the expression of feelings. The therapist needs to hold in mind the importance on the one hand that the expression of feeling is central to psychological insights, while on the other hand protecting the couple from the potential destructiveness of uncontrolled attacks. Rules about not hitting below the belt or the limit to what is allowed between partners provide some of this containment in the therapeutic context. It is vital for the therapist not to unconsciously allow the couple to act out the therapist's own unresolved difficulties concerning relationships. Being aware of counter-transference responses will help in this regard, especially to note feelings such as irritation, boredom, over-protectiveness, tiredness and helplessness, which may indicate that the therapist has been unconsciously drawn into the process between the couple.

Confidentiality is another central aspect in creating a safe working place for couples. This refers to the usual boundaries of confidentiality that therapists and counsellors provide for clients. This implies not divulging the identity of the couple as well as any of the information arising in the sessions. Further the therapist needs to develop a process for dealing with secrets and confidential information in the system. In a conscious or unconscious attempt to triangulate the therapist, one of the partners may try to draw the therapist into a shared secret. A frequent example involves secret information about the existence of another relationship, an affair or the so-called 'third party'. It is important, at the outset of the therapy, to make it clear that the therapist cannot hold secrets and that whatever information is shared, for example by letter or over the telephone, will become part of the therapeutic system. Otherwise therapists will find themselves handicapped and unable to move freely to provide the necessary unbiased mediation. Such an attempt to engage the therapist without the knowledge of the other partner does, however, reveal important information about the dynamics of the system. For example, it may point to the couple's constant attempts to seek adjudication or support outside of the couples system, which may currently be experienced as 'dangerous' or 'unfair' by one or both of them. Further it illustrates how crucial it is for the therapist to remain open and sensitive to the individual's dynamics, whilst at the same working hard to avoid colluding with one person or an issue. The strong pull to take sides may indicate the need for one or both partners to have a separate and private therapeutic place in which to work out their own intrapsychic conflict safely (to do their own work).

Continuing the theme of a safe and contained environment, a further issue is related to making good clear contracts. The therapist in clarifying his/her role also stipulates the limits and commitments of this kind of work. In the section on contracting above, we have described how this process is used in such a way that it serves as the basis for developing negotiating skills. The contracting phase, by revealing the patterns of communication and some of the dynamics in the relationship, allows for the therapeutic work to begin immediately. In the contracting phase the partners reveal their capacities to think about why they have sought help, what they need and want, what their expectations are and how they see and define the issues. This process provides a good deal of information about their ability to think, to negotiate, to compromise and indicates the realistic nature of their goals, aims and expectations. We also stress the contractual process as a helpful skill for couples to learn and to integrate into the ongoing fabric of their everyday lives. This will allow for the transfer of learning from the therapy into other contexts and provide them with a basis for negotiating successfully. In this way, the sense of containment provided by the therapy can become an enduring feature of their interactions in daily life.

EMPATHIC LISTENING

We believe that listening skills are central not only to the therapy process but to the creative development and maintenance of any intimate relationship. In the role of mediating the problem-solving capacities of the couple, the therapist's most potent tool is empathic and skilled listening. Not only is this a central technique for gaining a real understanding of the overt and covert issues, but it forms a very good model for the partners to adopt in their relationship with each other. The experience of being listened to with empathy and concern may be unusual and therefore underdeveloped in one or both members. Even if empathy is present in relation to certain issues, people may be less tolerant of the expression of needs and feelings which they themselves suppress or consider of minimal importance.

The importance of empathy in the therapeutic relationship has been extensively discussed. Since Carl Rogers' description of empathy as one of the core conditions (Rogers, 1951), its use has been emphasized in diverse approaches to counselling and psychotherapy as well as in the teaching of listening skills in other settings. Empathy can be defined as 'understanding so intimate that the feelings, thoughts and motives of one are readily comprehended by another' (Morris, 1981, p. 428). It is important for the therapist not only to understand but to be able to communicate the empathy. This communication involves the therapist in sending the empathic message as well as the client's experience of being understood. It is not the same as literal reflection, a simplification of the client-centred approach, or as necessarily agreeing with the client. Rather, it involves conveying to a person that the essence of their unique subjective experience is understood by another.

The experience of being understood is very potent and opens the way for clients to express unacknowledged and even unknown needs and feelings. As these are heard by the therapist, they can be more fully understood and worked with. Having the partner there as part of the process is particularly potent and moving when deep unexpressed needs are authentically revealed for the first time. Such an experience can be extremely reparative for a person who has for many years regarded their needs and feelings as sources of shame, rather than as a part of their essential core self. In this situation rather than the therapist drawing the emotional energy by using themselves in the transference, they can mobilize the partner to provide the contact and intimacy in the present. This may involve an intervention such as: 'What do you feel Roger, when Cynthia says she is angry with you?'; 'What do you feel Jemma, when Jay talks of his love for you?' The therapist places herself in the role of the facilitator of the process between the partners, to which her own relationship with each of them is secondary. By such a process, she can gradually enable the two people to re-engage in intimate dialogue. This stance requires a minimising of any transferential feelings for the therapist by dealing with these openly in the session and then redirecting the energy into the couple's relationship. In this sense, the role of the therapist is to facilitate the process between the clients, and not to work with each individual as a separate entity. We sometimes describe this process by saying 'the client in this case is the couple's relationship', and not the individuals per se.

The longed-for understanding and contact provided by an empathic stance is central to what people seek in intimate relationships. This is the opportunity to practise in order to create intimate contact in their external lives and outside of therapy. It becomes remarkably apparent that far more important to people is the experience of being deeply understood than necessarily agreed with. When a couple's early experience involved the belief that it is important to win, or to be right at all costs, they will believe that it is not possible to be understood in a close relationship. In these situations, the experience of empathic listening conveys something central to them about relating and relationships. Kahn (in Kahn *et al.*, 1989, p. 217) notes 'that anger and hostility occur as responses to lapses of empathy in all human relationships.' Anger at empathic failure can lead to creative discussions and reparative opportunities. The expectation is not that people will always get it right, but rather that they will be prepared to acknowledge when they have not understood, apologize and remedy the misunderstanding.

The reactions to being missed or not heard range from anger and fury to disappointment and sadness. Being misheard pushes people into their old adaptations, which were developed as defences or protections against the psychological pain of not being seen. Much of the hurt and miscommunication and misunderstanding between couples revolves around their empathic missing of each other. Thus in defining the sessions as an opportunity for understanding as well as learning how to listen fully, the notion of empathic listening becomes both a tool and a method in this process. It has an auto-therapeutic quality while, at the same time, it opens the way for couples to change something in their style of communication as they understand the value of empathic listening. They can then transfer this skill into their relationship outside of the sessions.

Berne says that 'in intimate love relationships, people talk to each other relevantly, directly, without distraction, and intensely.' (Berne, 1963, p. 195). The therapist needs to model this way of communicating by interacting like this in the sessions. At the same time, in order to keep the thinking process active, the therapist monitors and modifies the emotional intensity of the interactions. Our understanding is that sensitive counselling and therapy involves monitoring and modifying interactions, by being more or less emotionally intense and at the same time remaining direct, relevant and task focused. The emotional intensity of the transactions evoke different developmental levels of experience. (Clark, 1991). This process will involve teaching people about a range of emotional expression appropriate in different situations, especially where they may only have encountered dramatic extremes of expression in their families of origin, or the polar opposite of this.

The empathic listening phase between partners may involve a number of prior steps. Many couples do not even hear the content or the words of the other because they are too busy formulating their reply, argument or defence. In such situations they frequently do not even wait for the other to finish but interrupt and may overtalk one another. ('You did not remember our wedding anniversary which tells me how little you care . . .' 'If you took the trouble to ask me where I was yesterday . . .' 'I'm not interested in your excuses so spare me those.')

As this process begins to unfold the therapist moves in, stops the interrupting partner to question what they have just heard, asking for repetition or reflection of the other's communications. When partners begin to realize that they will get their chance to speak, and be given the opportunity to think about and express their view, which will be taken seriously, they start to relax, slow down and find the capacity to listen to the other and think about what they are saying. This in itself can be a powerful learning experience.

As therapists create these opportunities for mutual understanding they are able to move to the next stage. Here the therapist creates the possibility for the couple to go beyond listening and reflecting to opening themselves up to be really impacted, moved and affected by each other. As they experience the opportunity to express their needs, deepest fears and shame and when they experience these being understood and accepted, perhaps initially by the therapist, they become able and willing to provide each other with the same possibilities.

This brief-term work then moves from creating the time and place for a process of empathic communication to a situation where affective bonds are strengthened and intimate contact deepened.

NEGOTIATING AND CONFLICT RESOLUTION

'Isolation, the failure or inability of partners to talk in an ongoing way about their respective concerns, appears to be at the root of most couples' problems.' (Wile, 1981, p. 200). A shared problem leads to a shared solution. In order to get agreement and problem resolution, it is essential that each partner agree on the definition of the problem as well as on the process of negotiation and resolution. Recognizing that an outcome may include agreeing to disagree may be relevant. Any good partnership, business or other relationship, relies on good negotiating and conflict resolving processes. Interestingly enough as these skills are being more and more emphasized in the work environment, many participants of such training courses recognize the relevance these skills have for their personal lives as well.

Couples need to understand that differences are natural and conflict is both inevitable and a part of normal living. If conflict is not addressed, the angry feelings may go underground and lead to an accumulation of resentments, which may undermine the couple in the long run. No one person can resolve conflict by themselves, since it is an interpersonal problem, and thus always contains at least two points of view. Conflict is resolved by the parties involved sitting down together and interacting. A positive outcome can only come about with effective communication on one hand, and honest intent on the other.

As couples work towards conflict resolution, the first message is that the problem lies in *not* having a mechanism or process for conflict resolution, not in differences *per se*. Further, that how the problems are dealt with determines the success or otherwise of the partnership. 'The problem, it often appears, is not the identified issue, but the isolation caused by not having a way of talking about it' (Wile, 1981, p. 201). This sense of isolation polarizes the partners so that over time they begin to feel as if they will never find a way through to one another again. The task of the brief-term therapist is to enable them to re-engage and develop new skills for conflict management.

Whatever the cause of the conflict, the feelings that it arouses have to be expressed and understood before people can move towards negotiation and resolution. The feelings occur in two instances; within the people in conflict and between the conflicting parties. As described above, the expression of the way we feel in a safe and protected environment frees up thinking and allows us to find new and creative solutions. The safety of the therapeutic environment provides an arena in which people can learn new ways to express their emotions.

Some conflicts are not immediately or readily resolved. However, we can choose an attitude towards dealing with them. For example if one partner's work takes her to another country, the other may not want to leave an existing job, lifestyle, friendship network and family connections. Creative solutions to such problems can be found when each partner experiences their needs as being taken into account and heard by the other. Such a resolution may need to be worked out over a period of time, but the essential ingredient that makes for a successful outcome is the good will of both parties and the willingness to consider a workable compromise.

In a similar way to our discussion about people's beliefs about change, so too their beliefs about conflict are pertinent. Individuals carry their own particular beliefs about fighting and conflict that will operate in their intimate relating ('I'd rather hurt myself than the person I love'; 'It is better to endure something that you don't like, rather than to face anger'; 'My angry feelings are so powerful that I'm afraid of destroying someone with them'). Do the partners believe that conflicts can be creatively managed and resolved and if so, how? How does each person understand the process of compromising and cooperating? The hope or belief about the success of these possibilities is a vital first step in a conflict resolution process. Then another number of steps need to be followed in such a process.

It is important to clarify the exact areas of difference. This clarification process demands clear thinking. What is the real nature of the conflict? People argue about things which cover up deeper fears. For example, an argument about coming home late for dinner may involve the suspicion of another relationship. Similarly, an argument about spending too much time at the gym may mask the partner's concern about the other's interest in another member of the same club. An argument about where to live, whether in the city or in the country, may cover a doubt about the ongoing viability of the relationship. An argument about a choice of wallpaper for the spare room, may really be about whether the one partner values the other's judgment in all matters. Initial exploration with the therapist may uncover the underlying hopes and fears that may need to be clearly spelt out before a particular area of conflict can be addressed.

Many of the underlying issues involve the feeling or experience by partners that the relationship is not prioritized by the other person. A frequent complaint brought to the couples therapist is that the partner 'spends too much time away from home' and does not give the relationship its due and proper place in their lives. This may be particularly true in second marriages where new partners feel children from previous relationships, work, parents, etc., all come first in the list of priorities and they are bottom of the partner's pile.

Once the management stage has been reached, it is important for the therapist to support clear adult functioning. Principles important for the mediator or therapist include staying calm themselves and avoiding being emotionally drawn into the argument. The therapist's calmness functions as a containment for each partner. The therapist, by expressing feelings in an adult way and staying focused on the task and the current issue, helps the process forward. If couples begin to repeat themselves or keep going back to old issues, it is helpful to intervene with: 'We've been through that. Now let's get on with what's new.' Of course it is possible that the repetition reflects the fact that something has not been understood or attended to either by therapist or other partner. In such a case, it may be necessary to ask: 'What are we missing that you keep repeating yourself?' Either way the process of repetition is addressed. Clear contracting about the focus of the discussion is essential, so that the area of conflict is defined and then addressed.

The recognition of feelings remains a central focus of the therapeutic process. In this regard it is useful to name feelings. The naming process is refined when central feelings are linked to the experiences that they reflect: e.g. sadness is related to loss and requires compassion; anger reflects frustration and the wish to have things changed or different and needs to be responded to seriously; whereas fear demands reassurance. These interventions provide the couple with a learning experience about the process and function of affect, which is frequently a deficit in systems of education.

The therapist, by creating the opportunity for each partner to be heard and responded to, as described above, allows each viewpoint to be expressed, explored and addressed. This is the stage that rests heavily on accurate hearing, and understanding, and relies on the listening skills perhaps newly developed in the sessions. The interventions here are variations of: 'What have you just heard X say about Y?' and 'What do you understand, think, feel about what has been said?' These interventions allow for checking and clarifying the communications. If a person 'feels understood and responded to', they are usually more ready to discuss a compromise and negotiate creatively. We have stressed how important it is for the therapist not to take sides, to support partners to accept that at times agreeing to disagree is also a solution. The centre of this process involves getting partners to understand each other. Understanding is more important than agreement and the issue is not about winning or losing. Even when agreement is not possible, it is nonetheless a valid goal to get people to the point of understanding that someone else could hold a different and equally valid view.

The most important task of the therapist as conflict negotiator is to observe and listen carefully both to the content and process of the interactions. Interventions should be short and to the point. Protagonists should be kept to the central issue. If the process appears to be getting out of hand, the therapist should stop it, and bring the couple back to the salient points.

In the end successful relationships depend on the ability of the partners to negotiate with each other and be willing to make compromises for the sake of the relationship. Most couples of course do compromise many things for the sake of the relationship. If these compromises are unrecognized or unacknowledged, however, resentments build. Bringing out the compromises partners feel they have made, as well as negotiating about new areas where it may be necessary for more compromise, eases tension and ensures a sense of fairness and recognition. Relationships cannot be dealt with on a 'this for that' bargaining basis where each partner keeps score and will only give in proportion to what they perceive that they 'owe' the other. ('I'm not prepared to listen to another complaint about the office . . . you still owe me something for entertaining your ungrateful boss . . .'). Yet some form of fair play is involved in the process of negotiating mutual need satisfaction. ('I'll take the children to the zoo this afternoon while you write your essay. Later I would really like to chat to you about the problem in the office . . .'). Partners' sense of sacrifice and compromise needs recognition, acknowledgement, reciprocity and gratitude from each other.

Good negotiating skills are invaluable in most situations as well as central to smooth relationships and partnerships. The format of this brief-term intervention allows for a good educative process in this regard. If people can negotiate well on behalf of their selves and their intimate issues, it will stand them in good stead in relation to other situations. In addition to needing the skills of good listening and reflecting, negotiation includes recognition, appreciation and acknowledgement. Recognition and acknowledgement are often the missing elements in people's interactions with each other.

A useful exercise, which is helpful in this regard, is encouraging people to express appreciations and resentments to each other in relation to a topic or issue. All too often people focus on the resentments and neglect to acknowledge the appreciations. Expressing both sides allows for a sense of completeness or closure on issues. ('I resent the amount of time and energy you spend on your work'; and 'I appreciate your sense of responsibility to our family'; 'I resent the time that you spend chatting to your friends on the phone'; and 'I appreciate the social network you have established in our new neighbourhood').

A central assumption that we adopt as therapists is that affective bonds are the primary motivators. However, people often feel ashamed of their deepest needs and feelings, therefore feeling compelled to protect themselves from experiencing this shame, as we have referred to elsewhere under the discussion of shame-based systems. Further, people will seek recognition at any cost to themselves, accepting negative interaction rather than getting no response at all. This may lead to endless unproductive fights and wrangles that at least provide some contact and interaction between them. The therapist's task is to support the partners in finding healthy ways of reaching out to one another.

According to the tenets of reinforcement theory, behaviour that is positively responded to is likely to be repeated. At times couples need reminding of these simple principles, particularly as behavioural changes begin to occur as a result of the work done in the therapy sessions. This desirable behaviour should be clearly supported and undesirable behaviour noticed, addressed and stopped. ('I appreciate that you have commented on the effort I took to get you the compact disc that you particularly wanted'; 'I feel hurt when you criticize my family in front of our friends'; 'I love the warmth in your voice when you greet me over the phone'; 'I feel upset when you ignore me for hours on end').

Couples may need to be reminded that even intuitive and sensitive partners are not able to read minds. The belief that love means that you intuitively know what the other person wants, likes and needs has undermined many a couple's intimacy. People need to learn in any relationship what pleases and what displeases the other; this information can then form the basis for negotiation about mutual need fulfilment. Assumptions should be checked and disappointments dealt with. ('But you know that I get hurt when you make jokes about my accent. Please do not assume that I share your sense of humour about the Irish. After all, Ireland is my country!'; 'I cannot guess when you want me to spend time with you; please let me know').

FAIR FIGHTING IN MARRIAGE

Fighting is so often associated with bullying, violence and abuse that people may lose a sense of the importance of being able to have a good fair fight about differences in order to retain the vibrance of a relationship. When people fight, they mobilize their energy in support of an issue that is important to them. Gestalt therapists maintain that expressing anger makes for good contact. This underlines the point that if I get angry with you, it means I have an investment in relating to you. Anger is a signal that a person wishes to change something in their world, that the other person matters enough to engage with in an energetic manner. It is when people have become indifferent to one another, that the prognosis for their relationship is not good. As long as there is energy and the will to engage with the other, there is hope that change can still happen. When we get angry with someone, we have a desire that the person change in some way towards us. If we can learn to express this clearly and directly, then there is a better chance that we will be really received and attended to by the other person.

In expressing anger, we teach people to refer to the specific behaviour that has upset them, and not to generalize to the other person's whole being. ('I get angry when you forget to do the shopping you agreed to do for the weekend' as opposed to 'You're such a slob, you just never get around to anything!') We understand that a good hearty fight may precede this; people may need to ventilate and express their grievances about an issue before they are open to negotiating changes in behaviour. At the point at which partners are ready to move forward, then a process as outlined above may prove helpful. The individual is encouraged to be specific both about the area of discontent and about the desired new behaviour, for example, 'I get angry when you . . . (specific behaviour), and what I would like you to do instead is . . . (desired change)' (Steiner, 1984). This does not put the onus on the other to change in the prescribed manner, rather it opens up the possibility of negotiating behaviour changes related to the specific request of the partner. The specified request provides material for discussion, compromise and negotiation. Such a deliberate and 'Adult' negotiation may be the end part of a 'fair fight' the nature of which is described in the following paragraphs.

In our work with couples, we have over the years evolved some parameters for 'fair fighting' in relationships.

1. Specify the issue: agree what the specific issue is that you are angry about and agree to stick to that issue in the course of the fight. If you have identified several contentious issues, you may need to arrange separate times to deal with all of them. Conflating several issues is not likely to lead to a resolution of any of them.
2. Choose a mutually suitable time: choose a time that suits you both and when you have enough time to deal with the issue. Do not start a fight just when one party has to go to work or the children are needing their supper!
3. Choose a suitable space: choose a room that is private, preferably not your bedroom, where you know that you will not be disturbed or disturb anyone else.
4. Listen to each other: shouting each other down may be minimally satisfying but will not lead to a successful outcome. Give the other person the opportunity to express their anger and have their say.
5. Do not drag in the past: stick to the particular issue that is the subject of the fight. Do not relate a catalogue of past sins and omissions that will cloud the present fight, however tempting that may appear.
6. Express anger, but do not resort to abuse, physical violence, blame or calling one another names. Blame and abusive labelling are discounting of the other person and unlikely to keep the fight 'clean'. In fact, an agreement not to harm the other person or yourself or damage the environment is a good starting point.
7. Stop if you cannot keep the communication straight: agree to stop if either of you feels that the fight is no longer straight and related to the specified issue. You can agree to resume again at a future time when you have both had occasion for reflection.
8. Agree to differ: having a good clean fight does not imply that you have to end up agreeing. You may, in fact, agree to differ and then later work out a compromise solution to the problem.
9. Agree to discuss a compromise: often what is required in a tricky situation is a creative compromise. When people have expressed their anger and voiced their disquiet, they may be more ready to negotiate a realistic and workable compromise.

These parameters have proved useful to couples particularly when they are 'learning' how to fight or where there is a tendency to conflate a number of issues into one fight or where people constantly dredge up from the past all the occasions that they have ever resented something or been angry about a slight or omission on the part of the other. Once the partners have adhered to these parameters a few times, albeit it in a somewhat stylized manner, fair fighting may become a habitual part of their relationship so that they do not need to formalize the encounter in this way any longer.

EXERCISES AND HOMEWORK ASSIGNMENTS RELATED TO PROBLEM-SOLVING AND CONFLICT RESOLUTION

Homework assignments grow out of the ongoing work of the session and relate directly to the contract that is the focus of the therapy. What we give below are some typical examples to give the flavour of what may emerge and be 'taken home' for further experimentation and practice. Homework assignments need to be agreed in consultation with the couple and are to be carefully graded to suit the stage of the therapy. If these factors are taken care of, then 'homework' can prove a very useful adjunct to the brief-term intervention.

1. What is a compromise? A useful homework assignment is to ask both parties to reflect between sessions on what they understand a compromise is. Does compromising mean first doing what one party wants, and then what the other desires? Does it mean that partners take turns in yielding to the other? Does it mean an attempt to meet half way so that each gets some of what they want but perhaps not all? Does it involve partners in finding another third alternative that pleases neither as well but is at least more desirable to both than the other's first choice? Such a discussion can open up the negotiating process between people and lead to an evaluation of some of their underlying assumptions about problem-resolution.
2. A useful exercise for a couple involves reflecting on their own problem-solving process by answering the following three questions. How did your mother solve problems? How did your father solve problems? How do you solve problems? What suggestions about changing your style of problem-solving would you give yourself if you were your own therapist? When presented with this

information people can come up with useful discoveries. ('I can see immediately that I do exactly what my father used to do. Worry about the problem on my own and then work out a solution without approaching anyone else for help unless I am desperate. If I were to advise myself about a change I would say: ask for help earlier in the process!')

3. Another helpful homework assignment is based on being specific about areas of anger and the related requests. Partners agree to practice using the formula 'I get angry when you . . . (specific behaviour) . . . because what I imagine is . . . (evaluation of the other's behaviour) and what I would prefer you to do instead is . . . (specify desired behaviour)'. This assignment is somewhat formal, yet it has proved useful in helping couples who have tended to 'dump' all the past history whenever they get angry and generalize in a way that is unhelpful and undermining. It also offers people the opportunity to 'air' some of the assumptions they have about one another that subtly influence their relationship on a covert level.

8

WORKING THROUGH THE AREAS OF INTIMACY, SEXUAL GRATIFICATION AND FUN IN RELATIONSHIP

In this chapter we will be discussing the capacity for intimacy in relationships. We consider that the partners' sexual relationship is often a barometer which reflects the other aspects of their intimate communication. The sexual problems and incompatibilities highlight the couple's way of dealing with intimacy, sentiment and close connectedness. Intimacy is an important goal in many relationships, though the couples therapist needs to respect differing levels of the need for closeness and intimate contact. Attitudes to love and intimacy are culturally mediated and may by some not be assigned the priority that modern western society accords them (at least as ideals.) Much of our media coverage suggests that intimacy is connected with romantic attachment and is automatically present or absent. Whilst we do acknowledge that we often experience a strong connectedness with another person at first meeting, we nevertheless maintain that to achieve intimacy involves an ongoing commitment to a real meeting with the other.

People's capacity for sharing feelings, expressing emotional needs and achieving closeness is shaped by their early childhood experience. In agreement with Stolorow and Atwood we embrace the idea that children develop a systems competence through the 'recurrent patterns of mutual influence between mother and infant' that serves to regulate their interactions in subsequent relationships. (Stolorow and Atwood, 1992, p. 23). We have discussed this process at some length in Chapter 3. Since this development takes place from a very young age, some of the principles regulating a person's relational capacity are unavailable to their current awareness. Characteristic interaction patterns will emerge between the partners in therapy sessions, particularly in relation to affect and need. For example, if someone has habitually shut down on their own emotions and affective needs, this will manifest in toned-down, flattened affect or in 'shoulds' that inhibit joy, sexual expression, fun and 'childlike' activities. Such inhibitions may then become the contractual focus of the brief-term therapy.

DEVELOPING INTIMACY

Mutuality and mutual exchange is a central component of relationship and, in our philosophy of couples therapy, forms the bedrock of both the therapeutic alliance and of the relationship between the partners. We are indebted to the work of Martin Buber and many contemporary writers and practitioners of gestalt therapy for their contributions about the importance of dialogue in relationship. Such a stance fits well with our stress on bonding in the early child–parent relationship as the basis for subsequent close relating. Buber (1994) mentions the concept of inclusion in relationship. He defines this as the capacity to enter into the life of the other, to experience the world intensely from the subjective view of another person. At the same time it involves retaining your own centre, staying in touch with your own experience. Inclusion involves the ability to move back and forth between these two positions of 'being centred in one's own existence, and yet being able to go over to the "other side"' (Hycner, 1993). This is to be distinguished from empathy alone: 'Inclusion is instead a turning of one's entire existence to the other and the concentrated attempt to experience the other person's experience as well as one's own. For Buber whereas empathy ignores one existential pole of the dialogue, in the true moment of inclusion neither side of the dialogue is ignored' (Hycner, 1993). It is important for the brief-term therapist to practise inclusion so that he enters into the perspective of each member of the couple and into their relationship experience, while at the same time retaining an awareness of his own process. This is a challenge of no small proportions and calls for a deep emotional and intellectual commitment on the part of the therapist. Yet we believe it is essential for the therapist to practise inclusion, not only for its healing properties but primarily because it is crucial to the couple to experience a modelling of mutuality in this way. The practice of inclusion, which can be consciously worked upon, opens up the way for truly intimate contact between two people. 'When two people show and express their true selves to each other in an attitude of I-and-Thou mutuality, a free flow of affective energy sometimes happens between them. This is possible when both give up controlling themselves and the other and allow Thou to happen. Buber says one can choose to act lovingly but cannot choose to feel love, that is something one allows to happen' (Yontef, 1993). The therapist does not impose mutuality and inclusion on the clients; rather she models and practises what she believes may assist the partners in developing intimacy. This will call upon a therapist to share of her own feelings in the therapy where these are relevant to the process of the work.

Intimacy in our view embraces the capacity for inclusion and is the cornerstone of good relationships. 'A relationship develops when two people, each with his separate existence and personal needs, contact each other recognizing and allowing differences between them. This is more than a combination of two monologues, but two people in meaningful exchange' (Yontef, 1993). Developing this mutuality in relationship involves a commitment to dialogue, a willingness to embrace the other's world, while living my own experience and a respect for individual differences. Inclusion is demanding and may be only momentary, but the experience will feed back into the closeness between people and strengthen the intimate exchanges between them. Our emphasis in Chapter 7 on empathic listening to the other is geared to helping people open up to the other's perspective and really 'hear' what is true for the other. The development of inclusion in an intimate relationship is even more challenging since it involves entertaining both my own and the other's perspective simultaneously, even if only for a few minutes at a time. Such a two-person view of any event will provide the persons concerned with a meta-level perspective which enables decisions that sensitively take into account the deepest feelings of both partners. This is what is aimed for on the process level in brief-term work with couples – to model moments of inclusion so that the partners are able to learn from this modelling and incorporate this stance into their relationships over time, even long after the therapy is over. We are the first to acknowledge that this is a challenge and for us constitues an ideal in relationship, not something we imagine happens frequently or without effort.

For the individual qualities which may enable a person to be intimate with another, we refer to E. Berne's definition of autonomy which comprises three capacities: 'The attainment of autonomy is manifested by the release or recovery of three capacities: awareness, spontaneity and intimacy' (Berne, 1964). He defines awareness as the capacity to really experience the world around us and to be open to that experience without being too influenced by others' interpretations of it. Such direct sensory experience will enable us to evaluate our experience for ourselves. To take Berne's concept a step further, if we can draw on our direct experience of our inner and outer reality, our thinking is more likely to be experience near, rather than derived from introjected beliefs and 'shoulds'. Spontaneity for Berne 'means options, the freedom to choose and express one's feelings from the assortment available' (Berne, 1964). In this sense spontaneity involves liberation from feelings we have been taught to have and re-accessing our own true needs and feelings. We would add to this that the release of spontaneity will also mean the release from shame-binds that have become associated with some of our basic organismic experience because such experience was not acceptable to others in our families or cultures of origin. Intimacy was described by Berne as 'the spontaneous, game-free candidness of an aware person' (Berne, 1964). This concept relates directly to our discussion in Chapter 3 of the 'vicious cycle' of interaction which may undermine communication, and therefore intimacy between people. Berne (1964) gave the name 'games people play' to such vicious cycles of miscommunication. In his therapy with couples he assisted the partners in analysing, understanding and finding alternatives to game-playing, so that they could experience intimacy. Our intention in identifying the central non-productive process of interaction in a couple's relationship is similar to this, and in line with what Erskine (1982) and Goldfried (1995) write about in their contributions to this theme.

THE IMPORTANCE OF PLAY IN INTIMATE RELATIONSHIPS

Much of the earlier discussion in this book describes the way intimate relationships can be improved and problems addressed where there is an investment both in resolution and enhanced intimate contact. We consider that play is an additional crucial ingredient in a successful and mutually satisfying relationship.

Play in adults can be understood as the opportunity for fun and shared enjoyment in the spontaneous expression of the core self. The emotional sharing and closeness of a core relationship at its best provides this opportunity for adults. If the intimate relationship does not create the environment for these important creative needs, the partners may be drawn to seeking these experiences outside the relationship. Since the capacity for creative expression is so closely linked to intimacy, experiencing it outside will change the nature and quality of the core relationship. The texture of the daily fabric of people's lives depends on some opportunity for creative space and self-expression.

In an important contribution to psychological thinking, D.W. Winnicott, the famous psychoanalyst and play therapist (Winnicott, 1989), describes the developmental process that underpins playing, creativity, true intimacy and contact. Winnicott describes the process of how young infants engage in the fundamental task of establishing an understanding of the shared external reality and the difference between inner and outer worlds. They take a toy, blanket, edge of a cushion or some concrete object that exists in the real world and they invest it with psychological or personal meaning. This object, known as the transitional object, usually represents some aspect of the mother or mothering, nurturing, security and warmth. The function of the transitional object is to provide a bridge between inner and outer reality which facilitates the development of the child's capacity for play. According to Winnicott's theory it is through playing that intimate communication occurs. Adults retain the need for such a safe transitional space in order to let go and relax from the demands of the external world. At the optimum such a safe transitional space is provided by the core intimate relationship in a person's life.

When young children feel safe and secure, they relax, experience the freedom to play, allow for spontaneity and express the real self. Where the environment is threatening or tense, children remain 'on guard', mobilizing a false self or adapted presentation in order to protect the real self. Winnicott thus describes the origins of spontaneity and authentic expression within the context of a 'holding' environment. He goes on to describe the capacity to play and to be alone which both occur originally in the presence of the mother. The expression of true self-experience occurs in the play space or the transitional space. The capacity for play, spontaneity and intimacy all rest on this early development. When adults have had sufficient security and holding in their early life, they will have a well-developed capacity for humour, resourcefulness and fun. Through their ability to express and experience their spontaneity, they will invite others to share this arena. Winnicott believed that true intimacy and contact occur in the overlap of two play areas. It is here that each can let go and share in a common transitional space.

Thus it is apparent that the capacity to grow and be enriched in a relationship depends on its life-enhancing and creative potential. People need to share in their most important and intimate relationships aspects of their real selves, the absurdity, the vulnerability, the humour and pathos of the human condition. Central to the quality of the relationship is the capacity to play together and to laugh together. The healthy aspect of mate selection includes finding a partner who enriches and enhances the person's life. However, naturally a balance is needed and relationships based purely on free child and spontaneous expression will flounder in the areas of life requiring responsibility, seriousness, thought and containment.

The therapist will seek out areas for shared experience and expression. In this arena it is helpful for therapists to be active and directive. It is necessary to explore areas in which partners share satisfaction and joy and direct them by way of tasks and homework to create those shared opportunities in their lives together. Therapist: 'So you have recognized the need to have time alone together to relax and play, doing something that gives pleasure to both of you.' Contracts and homework tasks that focus on time spent together and on enjoyable activities that couples share can gradually open up or extend this dimension of the relationship. An interesting difference between partners often emerges in discussions of where to go on holiday together and how to spend their time on holiday. Some people prefer active holidays where they can go sight-seeing, attend the theatre, visit galleries, or go on walking or climbing expeditions. Vigorous activities may well constitute their idea of 'fun and relaxation'. Others, in turn may prefer more 'lying around and chatting and reading'; for them a holiday at the beach where they can lie in the sun and relax may be the ideal. If people with such different tastes are in relationship, some creative negotiation and compromise may be required. (Examples from sessions: 'I may as well shut myself up in my own kitchen, put the stove on full heat and use a sand blaster to cover myself with fine sand – that would give the same effect as going to the beach and cost a great deal less!'; 'Climbing a mountain holds no attractions for me; I want to relax on holiday. If I want to work hard during my vacation, I may as well decorate the spare room. At least that way I will see some results for all that spent energy!') Such differing preferences will need to be clearly acknowledged so that the partners can negotiate a resolution that does not end up in bickering, alienation or competitiveness.

Because of the very different balances in intimate relationships, some couples will be very effective at problem-solving and caring for one another, but the play dimension may be slight or even missing from their repertoire. For others it may well have been their playful interaction that fuelled their coming together, and they may need to focus energy on developing skills in conflict resolution or the management of everyday realities in the home. Such differences will emerge in the initial assessment and become clearly etched in the process of the therapy shaping the contracts for change between partners.

SEXUALITY: REVOLUTION, EVOLUTION OR DISASTER?

The sexual arena not only reflects the status of the relationship but is also the area in which problems are most dramatically revealed and enacted. We live in a culture and in a society that stresses sexuality, sex appeal and the right to complete sexual gratification. Our advertisements and media relying on this emphasis on sex, imply that buying certain products, drinks or cigarettes will enhance people's sex appeal. So, on the one hand, we in the western world are bombarded with sexual stimuli, whereas on the other hand, we still come from a culture and religious upbringing which for generations has induced fear, shame and criticism around the open and spontaneous expression of sexuality. Thus the sexual revolution contains not only mixed messages but also myths. This is an arena in which we have not caught up with ourselves in developing new guidelines which are in line with the demands of our environment.

In the sexual area couples may feel very vulnerable and threatened. The climate of sexual permissiveness, the freedom with which men and women move, work out of the home and travel, provides many opportunities for sexual exploration and infidelities. Since the 1960s the widespread availability of contraception and the lessening influence of religion has decreased the taboos and increased promiscuity and infidelity, somewhat tempered by the advent of the HIV virus. The 1960s also saw, in the more permissive sexual climate, a variety of sexual experiments in relationships such as group marriages or so-called 'open' marriages. Many people in the west today also describe the pattern of their relationships as serial monogamy. Certainly 'till death do us part' is not an invarying part of a modern notion of marriage and the vows and promises that many couples make to each other have a different connotation.

The issue of fidelity is one that is likely to be confronted by couples living in this climate of sexual freedom. There are of course some cultures where having affairs is informally sanctioned as long as the family is kept intact. Various other solutions have also been tried out, in the complex society that we live in. One way or another many couples have consciously or unconsciously accepted the possibility that they or their partner will be involved in other intimate relationships. However, where there are already problems and where the affectional ties and bonds or the issues of trust are at stake, sexual fidelity may become a crucial issue and the focus for what is wrong in the relationship.

Many people are able to decide to give up their sexual freedom in the service of preserving the trust and openness in the relationship. This choice does involve couples in risking commitment and closeness. Once trust has been broken in a relationship, it takes a good deal of psychic energy and commitment to heal the rupture. One of the difficulties encountered by people who begin relationships while still in unresolved other partnerships is the underlying worry that each has about the other's capacity to cheat.

In the end, the best way of addressing these complex and potentially painful issues is as openly and honestly as possible. However, on these issues therapists will need to use all their own sensitivities and skills in understanding how far to go and with what degree of openness these issues can be thought about and addressed. Therapists will need to be clear about their own position on these issues so that their assumptions do not interfere with the couple's prospect of resolution.

Many relationships suffer from sexual problems and the partners may benefit from a referral to a sex therapist who specializes in problems of this nature. Here, however, our notion of the sexual relationship as a barometer of the relationship is important. Often sex is the issue that first brings people into therapy or to seek help. They may have already resorted to sex therapy or some other source of help for these difficulties. The most common problems that affect men are connected to loss of erection or premature ejaculation and with women inability to achieve orgasm. Sexual inadequacy in either partner usually leaves both with a sense of inadequacy and disappointment. Although couples may claim that holding and physical contact is enough, this may be a way of avoiding what is missing in their sexual lives – not to minimise the importance of affectionate touch. But the sexual problem may also mask deep-seated communication difficulties that affect all areas of the relationship. These may fall well within the scope of the brief-term couples therapist.

Sexual issues and the pain they evoke can be greatly relieved if they are sensitively and openly explored. Therapists need to be comfortable with their own sexuality as well as not having a rigid set of rules about the rights and wrongs of situations. In an open and accepting frame many pertinent issues such as couples' attitudes to sex, what these are in their families, cultural expectations, partner's behaviour (verbal and non-verbal) can be relevant. Of further significance could be people's adolescent experience, previous partners and overall sense of self-esteem.

A striking fact to emerge in recent years is the widespread occurrence of some form of sexual abuse in childhood, particularly among adults with psychological problems. Sometimes these incidents are not only unreported but even unremembered. Nevertheless their effects can be widespread, long lasting and damaging to subsequent sexual relationships. Where sexual traumas such as abuse, abortion, losses and miscarriages can be recognized and spoken about in sessions, relief and healing can occur and be shared in the relationship. We have frequently dealt with couples where one partner is suffering from the symptoms of a delayed and untreated post-traumatic stress disorder. A focus in the brief-term therapy will then be dealing with this unresolved trauma and grief, enabling the other partner to support and understand the dynamics as they affect the relationship. At times, of course, the trauma has involved both people and the debriefing and dealing with feelings associated with the event will involve both sides.

There are situations where it is productive to explore people's sexual fantasies and secret desires. Sexuality, sexual expression and sexual desire is fraught with the potential for shame and guilt. Consequently many of these aspects may be unacknowledged. Loving each other involves knowing about and meeting each other's needs. Partners need to be given a safe space in which to articulate needs and fantasies that may be able to find their expression with the partner once that person possesses the knowledge. There may be fears that certain fantasies or desires are shameful or repulsive to the other. In these cases, skilful talking, negotiating and compromising, as well as sensitivity, is demanded of the therapist. In contradistinction, where there is compliance to a sexual practice that causes damage or psychological distress, in the long run its continuation will only undermine the relationship.

Withholding sex is a common tactic used to gain control and power in the relationship, or to express anger. Partners may differ as to the frequency with which they desire sex and this may then form the content of a process by which they manipulate one another. This is an area that frequently arises in the relationship assessment and will form the material for discussion and compromise. Couples who have young children, and/or other stresses and demands in their lives, may find themselves unable to relax and enjoy sex. Thus the frequency, the when, the where and the how of sex may all come into the negotiating arena. Couples need help to prioritize their relationship and encouragement to find time and space for privacy and relaxation together. In busy lives with multiple demands, such times may become rare or be squeezed out altogether.

In the over-burdened and stressed lives that many adults live, in which they have multiple roles and responsibilities, couples need to negotiate around time and space together. A fairly common example of one of the issues that needs negotiation would be where one partner has children from a previous marriage. This parent needs to devote time and energy to these children, which will be experienced as 'subtracted' from the present relationship. A complicating aspect could be guilt about these children.

Where a new partner comes into an existing situation, they may very quickly experience themselves as low on the other's list of priorities. It is of course essential that issues such as these be brought out in the open and discussed. The other parent may feel that they are doing their very best to keep everyone happy, although in the end may not be succeeding with anyone. At times family sessions for these issues could be useful.

In this area, whether it is around step-children, shared and individual responsibilities, sexual difficulties and tensions, the straight talking and negotiating skills that are being developed through the process of the brief-term work can be fruitfully employed. In this regard the capacity for 'inclusion' discussed at some length above provides an important bridge to understanding and mutually satisfactory agreements.

RELEVANT EXERCISES AND HOMEWORK ASSIGNMENTS

Homework assignments or agreements to focus on a particular task related to the overall contract of the brief-term therapy grow naturally out of the sessions. What we give here are some characteristic examples or possibilities to give the flavour of the type of assignments that are explored at home and brought back to the subsequent session for evaluation and discussion. We stress this aspect lest the reader get the impression that homework is given by rote or is extraneous to the ongoing life of the couple.

An Awareness Exercise

We are again indebted to Stevens (1971), from whom we derive this exercise.

1. The partners are asked to spend about 10 minutes at a time sharing the awareness of their experience with the other. This can take the form of completing three sentences: I am aware that I . . . ; I am aware that you . . . ; I am aware of avoiding . . . , and then letting the other person do the same. This can be completed several times in the allotted time and often has the effect of bringing people closer together as they get an insight into the other's ongoing awareness process.
2. Developing areas of fun together: partners can be asked to think back to what they enjoyed and found to be 'fun' as children. Then

they can consider if there are any related activities that they would like to share in the present. This exercise led to one couple taking up cycling together and exploring the countryside on their expeditions; another couple discovered a shared passion for the game of 'Scrabble' and have enjoyed relaxing in this way at the end of the day.

3. Surprise one another: a task that can lead to new discoveries is an agreement to surprise one another with something that you believe will be fun for the other from your knowledge of that person.

4. A role reversal exercise can also be very revealing for couples. Partners can take each other's positions on a subject and express what they believe to be the other's point of view. This offers a rich opportunity for developing a closer understanding. We would suggest, however, that an exercise of this kind which usually evokes sensitive material be done the first time in the presence of the therapist so that partners can have access to mediation and facilitation should they get into difficulties.

9

WORKING THROUGH THE ISSUES RELATING TO CARING FOR THE OTHER

In many ways much of what we have already described and covered in the various sections comes together and is integrated in this section. Our earliest experiences and deepest needs in intimate relationships are connected to our wishes, longings, and fantasies of being taken care of by a loving person. Some of the deep needs that emerge between couples are those that we as therapists and counsellors recognize in our patients and clients – needs for recognition, acknowledgement, holding, containment, respect and understanding.

The caring dimension is one of the crucial aspects in a close relationship. Our most significant needs are those to feel seen, recognized and cared about. Our earliest and deepest experiences as children will determine our capacity for both caring and being cared for. It is not only important for children to experience their parents' love and respect, but also for them to express their love and caring and have it met and received. It is in this arena that the health or otherwise of individuals is really revealed. People who have not been cared for, who have grown up in abusive, neglectful and deprived circumstances lack the capacity and understanding to be able to be nurturing to themselves or others. The empathy and respect that the therapist conveys to each partner provides a good model of a way of being in a relationship and reveals aspects for the others to see and understand through this process. However, if there is a serious deficit in this area and people do not show a basic respect for the other's wellbeing, brief-term work may not be the therapy of choice. In such cases, a slow and long-term re-education process may be required.

BALANCING THE PARENTING DIMENSION

From a transactional analysis perspective, caring for each other can be seen as a function of the parenting capacity of each partner for the other. In good relationships, it is important that the parenting role is shared and each partner is capable of being nurturing and containing of the other's vulnerabilities and stresses. In practice, however, relationships may be unbalanced. One partner may be habitually in the parent role and the other in the child. In traditional marriages, this skew is along classic sex and gender lines. Women go from being daughters to being under the husband's protection and jurisdiction. Even recent legal documents had phrases like 'assisted by her husband' under a wife's signature and needed the husband's signature and authorization. Many marriage and divorce acts in western countries have only of late recognized an accrual system and a fairer distribution of assets among marriage partners. A further complication is that in addition to formal roles and positions, often there are secret contracts between partners that include unspoken agreements to look after or not abandon 'the child' in the other. Cultural beliefs usually put the wife in the role of the mother and hence as the nurturer or carer. However, we have dealt with many couples where the husband is in the position of the nurturer and carer and the wife does not reciprocate. Such an unbalanced relationship may be described as an unhealthy symbiosis, where the lack of mutuality often brings the couple to therapy. As these deeply embedded expectations break down, it is important to understand what thoughts and feelings about being cared for are being held by each partner.

In a related dynamic, both people may be competing for the 'parenting' role in the relationship. This dynamic can be summarized as 'I can care better than you can'! In such a process both people are avoiding the dependent role, the role of the cared for, needy and the 'given to' in the relationship. This is frequently the result of a family dynamic in which the person has been 'parentified' and had to take care of a depressed caretaker in order to survive themselves. Feelings of neediness and vulnerability had to be submerged in caring for the other. No wonder then that this person will find it hard to let go and allow himself to be cared for and cherished by another. A tendency to hide vulnerable and needy feelings may also be endorsed by a culture, especially one like the English culture that places a high value on 'being strong' and 'keeping a stiff upper lip'.

A variation of this dynamic was met by one of the writers in her couples practice. Kurt operated a debit and credit account system in his intimate relationship with Bart. He listed everything that Bart ever did for him or any present that Bart ever gave him, and then reciprocated exactly in the same measure, not a drop more or less as closely as he could calculate. He even took presents back to the shop at which they had been purchased in order to establish the exact price, and would then spend precisely the same amount on Bart's birthday present when that event came around. Problems arose because Bart did not subscribe to this finely balanced system, indeed he was not even aware of its existence. When the therapist did some deeper exploration into the dynamics underlying Kurt's debit-and-credit system of dispensing love and care, she discovered that he had been on the receiving end of a father who constantly expected him to be 'grateful' for what he had, and to behave in desired ways in order to show his gratitude. On one memorable occasion, Kurt's father had threatened to commit suicide if Kurt was not 'a good boy'. Kurt there and then decided that in his subsequent life he would never again owe anyone anything, down to the last penny. When Kurt revealed this experience in the therapy, Bart and the therapist were deeply moved and were able to convey their compassion to him. From then on, Kurt was able to consider the possibility of a relationship in which there could be more spontaneous shows of love, affection and caring without putting him under the heavy obligation he feared on the basis of his past experience. Individual exploration of the kind undertaken with Kurt has a place in brief-term therapy, as long as the mutual goal is served by this. The partner who witnesses such work often finds the process deeply moving and it opens up a new dimension that influences their perception of the other's intentions and behaviour.

At moments of stress, conflicting expectations about what is 'love' and 'care' may surface. A simple example will illustrate this discrepancy in expectations: in Sean's family people who were ill were left alone to recover in a darkened and quiet room; in Dawn's family, ill members were regularly visited with cups of hot tea or soup; brought flowers to cheer them up; and even the cats and the dog were included in the solicitous visits. Imagine how overwhelmed Sean felt by this 'unwelcome' attention at his first bad bout of flu. Equally Dawn felt 'neglected' and 'abandoned' when she fell ill and was left alone in a darkened room for hours on her own by Sean who was working at home at the time.

The therapist will facilitate partners to express how they wish and like 'to be cared for' so that this information is available for the other's consideration. This is an important area for clarification. Any couple's therapist has dealt with couples who have gone along for years, sometimes even half a lifetime, believing that certain behaviours pleased and were 'required' by the other, only to find out in the course of therapy sessions that this is not true. The other partner may have held back from telling the truth for fear of hurting their spouse. An intervention that may assist here is to ask each person to describe what 'caring' means for them and then to check out this list with the other person. This can then form the basis for contracting for the future. It is important for partners to check out in this way with each other what specific forms of care and nurturing they each desire and value. It is easy to assume that things were done 'the right way' in our families of origin and that everyone means the same by words like 'love', 'care', 'concern' and 'understanding'. Thoughtfulness and small gestures of love and respect are the daily contact points that make for quality in relationships. When someone knows, anticipates and cares enough to meet needs unasked or makes small but significant gestures of concern, the recipient feels supported and respected. These aspects serve to cut through some of the loneliness and alienation that people feel in a modern urban environment.

UNCONSCIOUS REPRODUCTION OF PAST PATTERNS OF PARENTING

A danger in intimate relationships lies in what has been articulated in psychotherapy as the theory of transference, projection and projective identification. As discussed extensively in Chapter 3, we inevitably bring into our current situation images and ways of organizing experience in close relationships from our previous experiences. Often this process is unconscious and outside our adult awareness. The vulnerability in any partnership lies in the tendency to parent in the way that I was parented, or expecting to be parented in a similar manner, as discussed in the previous section. Sometimes there is a hope that this time I will have found a better parent. Exploring these projections and understanding how the ghosts of the past interfere with the here and now are central in addressing this aspect of the relationship. The example of Kurt in the previous section amply illustrates this point.

The mechanisms of projection and projective identification operate very powerfully between couples. In intimate relationships we inevitably project aspects from previous relationships into the here and now. Particularly aspects from the family of origin will be brought into the new family being created. Partners will be seen to have characteristics of parents and/ or siblings or other significant features from the past. Where powerful projections dominate, the person who is the receiver of the projections may well behave in the manner expected as a result of the unconscious processes between the partners. This potential for picking up and acting out in terms of the projection is known as projective identification. Projective identification is a familiar dynamic for psychodynamically aware therapists, but is a more complicated and confusing dynamic for couples to manage. In the brief-term work described, an astute therapist needs to look out for, monitor and help the couple understand their projections and the way in which projective identification may operate between them. Taking a literary example may help here. Hamlet's bizarre behaviour has a powerful effect on Ophelia because of her attachment to him. When she goes mad, Hamlet's sanity reasserts itself and it is Ophelia who pays the price for it by killing herself.

BELIEFS RELATED TO CARING FOR ANOTHER OR BEING CARED FOR

In this section it is important to consider beliefs about needs, asking for things and giving to each other. Many people feel if you have to ask for something it is not worth having. Another myth is that 'if you really loved me, you would know what I needed.' Of course mind reading and knowing exactly what another's expectations and assumptions are is not always possible or a measure of the care and love involved. For example, Mary-Lou arrives home exhausted from a demanding day at the office exacerbated by a traffic jam on the way home. She finds Costa relaxing with his feet up at the television having arrived half an hour earlier than Mary-Lou. Mary-Lou is very hurt by Costa's 'casual' greeting while he is absorbed by a TV programme; she feels 'ignored and rejected' since Costa has not guessed how tired she is from wrestling with the traffic at the end of a difficult day. He is surprised by an unexpected attack from her when his behaviour is not unusual and some discussion yields the information that she is feeling vulnerable after her experiences and would have wished him to 'mind read' her need for greater attention and care.

We often give others what we would really like or want for ourselves, sometimes in the mistaken belief that this way they will recognize our needs and meet them. None of this is a substitute for direct expression of needs and a willingness to negotiate and compromise on these. The capacity for nurturing and care comes from having been well looked after and nurtured ourselves. All too often people have grown up in circumstances that were not nurturing so that they have not internalized or developed consideration towards others or patterns of caring that feed a relationship.

People may form a relationship with someone who is very warm and nurturing with the secret longing and desire to get the nurturing/ parenting they did not receive as a child. However, as the relationship develops and the need for parenting is met, the person may begin to feel restless and that they have outgrown the need for being looked after in a dependent role. At this point one of the partnership may start to complain of feeling bored, smothered or claustrophobic. There is often a loss of sexual attraction at this stage. The more the person fits a parental image or role the less attractive they become as a lover or sexual partner. Men seek sexual relationships with younger women for other reasons as well, like confirming their masculinity and potency and denying their own ageing. Women usually stay married to older men (father figures) but may seek affairs with younger partners to provide variety and sexual experience in their lives.

EFFECTS OF EARLY TRAUMA OR DEFICIT ON THE CARING DIMENSION

In their interesting article on couples' counselling, Boyd and Boyd (1981) identify caring as one of the central aspects to be identified and addressed with couples. In diagnosing and treating dysfunctioning in the realm of caring, they mention that the therapist is liable to observe one of the following patterns: On the one hand a high level of mutual discounting by partners of the other's needs and feelings; or alternatively while one partner discounts, the other is passive and does nothing to challenge this behaviour; or finally, passive disinterest and disrespect for the value and wellbeing of each other. When these processes are marked and serious, they indicate a high level of disturbance in one or both partners. They comment: 'It has been our experience that couples with caring component dysfunction initially chose each other on a basis of major script issues and personal pathologies' (Boyd and Boyd, 1981, p. 144). Where this is the case, i.e. there is an indication of serious pathology on the part of one or both partners, couples may need to decide whether there is a basis for them to continue in the relationship or not. Sometimes the damage in the current relationship is already so far-reaching that one or both people do not have the heart to continue.

Where couples come from very damaging circumstances, we must agree with Boyd and Boyd (1981), there is invariably the need for individual work, often of an intense and in-depth nature. In the case of the so-called 'personality or character' disorder, their loose boundaries and capacity to act out can be experienced as frightening and unmanageable by a partner. In this regard, it is important to remember that couples usually select each other, consciously or unconsciously, at their own level of pathology. By that we mean that even when there appears to be a mismatch in terms of the psychological functioning of the individuals, this should be more carefully investigated. For example when one partner appears to be the hard-working respectable member of society and the other is labelled 'mentally ill', it is wise to hold in reserve the possibility that the dysfunction may rest on both sides. The case of the unhappy and secretly battered wife of the seemingly well-functioning husband is an all too familiar phenomenon.

We also find that certain psychological needs and processes are very compatible with one another. We are referring here, for example, to the well-known complementary match between so-called 'borderline' and 'narcissistic' phenomena. Borderline features include an oscillatory dynamic between a need for closeness, which can be seen as a fear of abandonment, and a fear of engulfment or intimacy. This push/pull leads to such individuals 'inning and outing' in relationships, i.e. they move towards getting very close and intimate, then get scared of the engulfment so they may abruptly withdraw. When they pull back too far, fearing the abandonment brings them back into closeness. In many ways an emotionally withdrawn or self-involved partner who cannot handle the demands of a fully mutual relationship is a very good foil for such a person. The person with the 'borderline style' of relating will not get really close because of the fear of engulfment; equally, they will not relinquish the relationship through the fear of 'abandonment'. As much as the 'borderline' partner will complain about the lack of emotional contact, at another level the equilibrium feels unthreatening and secure. The person with a 'narcissistic style' often also chooses a dependent partner who clings to the relationship. Here the unspoken agreement may be 'as long as you flatter me and support my grandiosity, I will look after you'. The dependent style sacrifices his/her own opinions and independent judgement, and receives care in return. The 'narcissistic style' receives unqualified admiration without a hint of criticism or disagreement (Delisle, 1988). Such an interlocking dynamic provides an equilibrium of sorts that may survive until one or other of the partnership wishes to opt out of the covert relationship dynamic in favour of a more mutual exchange.

THE IMPORTANCE OF AFFIRMATION IN RELATIONSHIPS

In considering caring we can also return to the issue of stroking and recognition. A knowledge of what strokes the other person values is important in our understanding of their needs. Caring for others is expressed by the way we stroke them and understand and hold in mind their need for recognition and acknowledgement from us. Real caring includes not only so-called positive strokes, i.e. affirmation, reassurance and support, but also the willingness to engage with difficult and painful issues, the 'negative strokes' of transactional analysis. Giving straight information and feedback has been addressed in the section on conflict resolution. It is as important for a partner to know what upsets me and what I do not like, as it is to have the information about what pleases me. That way people have the information on which to base their choices. In our view, this knowledge of preferences and areas of vulnerability does not place either person under an obligation to please the other, but does provide them with the information relevant to the option they choose for action. If a person acts without this information, they may unwittingly miss the other person – a process that can continue for years of unsatisfactory exchanges. We believe that possessing the relevant information is a better option even if the decision is to act in a way that the other may not like. At least this can then be done in awareness with the full acknowledgement of difference and is overt in the relationship.

An essential task in this work is to help couples explore what they need from each other and to help them figure out how to get these needs met.

'What can I do this week to make your week go a little bit better or make you feel more loved, valued, appreciated?' (Bader and Pearson, 1988, p. 26)

A couple's way of handling this question reveals a good deal about the partnership, the partner's self-definitions, their ability to give and take, in addition to identifying the couple's developmental stage. Reciprocity in the dimension of caring is the goal of the work described in this chapter. At times, we may collude with another to keep them comfortable. When we do this often and do not confront the difficulties, we avoid real contact and play each other's games. Under the therapist's scrutiny, it becomes easier and more possible to become aware of what is attended to and what is ignored in the relationship. Thus couples can be helped and supported with the painful aspects of their style of communication and the interactions between them.

EXERCISES AND HOMEWORK ASSIGNMENTS ASSOCIATED WITH STRENGTHENING THE CARING DIMENSION

In this section we will give a few samples of homework assignments or exercises that may grow out of the therapeutic work along the dimension of caring. Again these are not intended for use in a random fashion; it is crucial that any exercises or homework assignments relate directly to the work in the sessions and to the overall therapeutic goals.

1. Information about caring: partners can be asked to create a list in which they complete the following sentence as frequently as possible: 'I feel loved when you . . .'. Partners can then exchange lists and gain an understanding of their very different needs and preferences about receiving love and care. This information can then be fed back into the relationship exchanges.
2. Specific contracts regarding caring actions have also proved useful in breaking through an impasse in this area, e.g. 'I agree to your request to sit down and talk about your day when I return from work in the evening' or 'I will hold you when you need comfort if you ask me clearly and directly'. Such contracts will have emerged from the material of the sessions.
3. Exploring how caring was expressed in our families and cultures of origin can often yield valuable information about areas of dispute,

especially in cross-cultural marriages. Relevant questions may include: How did your family behave when someone was upset? How did you express love and care for one another? Did family members express physical affection? Was caring the woman's function? Or did the men also assume a caring role? Was there a gender difference in how caring was expressed? An appreciation of individual and cultural dimensions of caring, elicited in this way, can lead to considerable insight into the other's frame of reference.

10

TERMINATION

In brief-term therapy, an awareness of the end is very much present from the outset. A sensitivity to the idea of the termination of the therapy will influence the process from its inception to its conclusion. This awareness of the time-limited nature of the intervention places constraints on the volume of work that can be attempted, yet the pressure of time also acts as an incentive for the participants to make the best use of the six to eight sessions at their disposal. The focused nature of the contracting and the very specific goals agreed upon serve to remind the therapist and the participants to consider the impending ending as a necessary containment for the process. In this sense termination is embedded in the process of the therapy from the outset, it influences all the interventions made by the therapist and keeps the three protagonists alert to the constructive and economical use of time.

Endings are often difficult and evoke memories of other experiences of loss, separation and abandonment. It is important to acknowledge the loss of the safe place which created the opportunity for empathic response and to allow for the feelings around endings to be fully expressed. This often takes the form of an expressed fear by the couple of 'managing on our own once the sessions end'. This is a natural response to the impending loss of the therapist's support and the containment provided by the therapeutic space. Once such feelings are given expression, then the couple can be supported to acknowledge their own strengths and coping abilities.

EVALUATION OF THE GOALS

As the ending approaches it becomes very important to undertake an evaluation of the goals agreed upon at the outset of the therapy. The initial question in this phase is what has been learnt and gained in the sessions. Asking this question helps the partners articulate and consolidate the gains achieved. Sometimes it is only as the learning is put into words that the gains become clear and this process then forms the basis for building a containing structure within which to sustain the new behaviour.

Partners can be invited to go over the sessions in their minds, highlighting the most significant moments. A useful question is to find out what each of them thought was most significant for the other. Usually there are key points in the work, in which important insights were gained or re-decisions made, that stand out as moments of change. Such moments will probably be charged with affect. Sometimes the therapist may be surprised, however, at the deep significance that an intervention may have had for one or both partners, which was not immediately evident at the time. For example: 'When you pointed out my belief that I'm not entitled to love unless I earn it by working hard to make sure that everyone else is happy, I suddenly saw how I then hold my partner responsible for guessing what I need!'

The discrepancies in partners' perceptions of significant learnings and the meaning attached to various discussions may also provide useful information. These discrepancies can point to the need for further work where more attention may be needed before the closure of the brief-term intervention in the final sessions. We know how strongly people's perceptions of events are coloured by their own frames of reference so that the partners may retain only that part of a session that best suited their own needs. If there are significant discrepancies about the meaning or value placed on certain points of discussion, these can be reviewed and clarified before closure. ('I remember that you agreed that we would move into a larger house!'; 'No, I said that I was prepared to consider a move, but needed more time to think through the implication!')

CONSOLIDATION OF GAINS

In situations where partners feel much has been gained and achieved, it is important for the therapist to both acknowledge and accept their gratitude and also celebrate with them the enhancement and enrichment of their relationship. The therapist may in this short period have become an important member of this 'family' and acknowledging the idealization is sometimes necessary in order to facilitate the termination process. Especially for people who may glide over the satisfaction phase of a process, it is important to celebrate, enjoy and savour the gains that have been made together. This will serve as good modelling for the future, so that due acknowledgement is accorded one another for small or large successes and changes subsequently made in the relationship. Occasionally partners may wish for some closing ritual that marks a new phase of their relationship with one another.

It is equally important to take up the disappointments and acknowledge what has not been solved or achieved. Even when people are doing their very best and working really hard, some pains are not possible to take away or cure. Sometimes, for example, the breakdown in relationship or the hurt caused by betrayal remains despite careful and sensitive acknowledgement. As already discussed, keeping couples together may not necessarily be the goal of the work. In some cases moving towards dissolution of the relationship may be the best solution. However, even in this eventuality, raising the issues and dealing with them in a safe and contained environment provides a better base for couples to separate and carry on with their future. The therapist can facilitate a creative process of disengagement if that is sought by the partners.

However, even when people decide to continue together, they may still be carrying the scars from previous hurts. In such instances, we may need to acknowledge that reconstruction and the healing process take time. New behaviours and contracts for ongoing change may do something to alleviate the anxiety about areas that still remain unaddressed or in need of healing.

Sometimes the impending termination evokes and provokes the need for 'more time'. It may be necessary to re-contract for an extra session to deal with what the termination evokes in cases where there have been multiple losses in people's lives. On the other hand, holding clear boundaries and understanding the meaning of trying to prolong the situation is also necessary for the therapist.

In certain cases, one of the outcomes would be for one or both partners to continue working individually in a more intensive or in-depth way, to deal with their early issues. These issues may have been uncovered in the brief work but there would not have been the opportunity to address them fully. Individual work will support the ongoing process of reconstruction in the couple's relationship.

REASSESSMENT OF THE CONTRACTS AND CONTRACTS FOR THE FUTURE

The most central aspect of the termination phase is the assessment of the agreed contract/s. Have these been met to the satisfaction of all parties? Are there observable indicators of change, both within the sessions and outside of these (as reported by the partners)? Have the partners gained an awareness of the process underlying their communication failures – of the cycle of reinforcement that perpetuates their non-problem-solving behaviour? Have they gained alternative options for more creative interaction that ensure straight communication of needs and feelings? Has the experience of new options within the sessions been generalized to situations outside of the sessions? These are some of the questions that are relevant at this point in the process. To ensure satisfactory closure, an assessment of the therapeutic contract/s is essential to therapist and clients alike.

In ending it also is important to look at the future contracts and what plans people have for sustaining the new behaviours and the changes made in times to come. Anticipating what could provoke old solutions and suggesting what alternative options exist is part of what the therapist will be doing at this stage. Where games have been named, dynamics uncovered and the meaning and function of behaviours understood, it is subsequently much harder for both partners to contrive to collude with each other and carry on the games. However, specific contracts related to processes that have been the focus of the work ensure a more likely positive outcome over time. (For example, a contract to ask clearly and directly for what one wants, can form the basis for continuing clarity of communication and avoid 'vicious cycles' of interaction.)

SAYING GOODBYE AND MOVING ON!

The final task for the couple and the therapist is to say goodbye. This ending may involve a final summary by the therapist of the gains made and support for the strengths in the relationship. Or it may involve some ritual that the couple have agreed with the therapist previously that symbolizes for them the changes that have been made and which has grown out of the process of the sessions themselves. One couple brought along a collage that they had jointly created since the previous session which portrayed in visual form both their achievements and their goals for the future. They took turns speaking on each of the changes, and then affirming their contracts for the future. This ritual was poignant for the therapist and the couple alike, since they had on arrival had severe doubts about the likelihood of continuing together due to accumulated resentments from the past. These were aired and addressed in the course of the therapy, freeing them to relate once again in an intimate and rewarding manner. Their final ritual illustrates this achievement.

Although the couple are aware that there is the possibility of a further six to eight sessions in the future, on negotiation with the therapist, it is vital that the brief therapy sequence be clearly and unambiguously closed by all parties concerned in it. The therapist will take the initiative in containing this process of creative disengagement. The therapist too needs the emotional closure of saying goodbye and 'letting go' of the clients. The partners can take the opportunity of saying their farewells to the therapist, whilst acknowledging both their appreciations and possible disappointments. It is important that the therapist allow the partners to take their leave of him and express openly their appreciation of the endeavour they have jointly undertaken. An open generous attitude on the part of the therapist will model for the couple the importance of both giving and receiving appreciation warmly and responsively in a relationship.

11

ETHICAL ISSUES

Couples therapy may raise ethical considerations over and above those posed by individual therapy. With three people involved in the process, the nature of the commitment and the process itself will inevitably be more complex than that of individual work. The therapist agrees to work with this couple's relationship and this primary commitment to the joint process will influence the interventions that the therapist makes. Even though the therapist may be tempted by or invited into doing individual work that is not directly related to this shared goal, it is important for the therapist to keep in mind at all times that it is the relationship 'between' these two people that is his concern. This is the task for which he has been engaged and is being paid by the couple, so this is the focus of the therapy. For this reason, the couples therapist needs to keep in mind that it is a system of two people that is his client, rather than two separate isolated individuals. The therapist's task is to intercede in the system in a manner that will unblock the communication and facilitate the system to operate more effectively. For some therapists this systemic focus is difficult to hold, because of their loyalty or predisposition towards the view of one or other of the partners. If this is the case, the couple is best referred elsewhere since it is of the essence of the couples therapist's task that he feels able to serve equally the interests of both parties. Where there is any doubt at all about this, the therapist is ethically bound to make an appropriate referral that will serve the joint needs of the clients.

Brief-term therapy with couples will pose similar challenges to any other brief-term work, where the therapist's time with the couple is circumscribed from the very outset of therapy. For these reasons it is important for the brief-term couples therapist to weigh up very carefully the ethical and professional boundaries of this work, as well as keeping in focus the inevitable constraints imposed by the time-limited nature of his brief with the couple. Not adhering to the parameters of the brief therapy may raise ethical issues related to the effective and appropriate delivery of procured services. Staying focused on the agreed goals requires a disciplined and well-planned approach on the part of the therapist who will need to select carefully from amongst his wide repertoire only those strategies and interventions that forward the goals agreed between him and the couple. Because of the in-depth knowledge of intrapsychic and interpersonal processes that is required in his training, the brief-term therapist is likely to be aware of complex dynamics operating in the couple's relationship which simply cannot be addressed within the boundary of the brief-term intervention to which he has committed himself with the couple. It is a challenge to the therapist to allow such insights to inform his practice, without imposing these on the couple in a way that does not serve their immediate goals.

The ethical principles outlined below refer specifically to areas of professional and ethical practice. However, we maintain that good ethical practice is closely bound to principles that underlie good therapeutic practice, which constitute the content of the previous chapters of this book. Adherence alone to specific ethical procedures does not ensure effective outcomes. This adherence to ethics needs to be underpinned by the commitment of the therapist to the therapy as a project that calls on all the skills, knowledge and expertise that he has accrued over the years of his training and experience as a professional. The ethical considerations discussed below, in addition to serving to protect the clients, will assist in promoting the therapeutic work by protecting the therapeutic space and allowing for clarity concerning the role of the brief-term therapist.

CONFIDENTIALITY

Confidentiality contracts need to be carefully negotiated. Partners will be assured that the fact that they are coming for help will be held confidential, as also any sessional information. Partners are, therefore, to be made aware that the sessions are confidential to the two of them and the therapist. Partners are advised not to contact the therapist individually between sessions to discuss material or to convey information 'that I don't want my partner to know, but I think it will help you to understand me'. People will sometimes attempt to do this by phone or by letter so the therapist is advised to spell out that any information conveyed in this way will not be regarded as confidential to the other partner involved in the therapy. The therapist is well advised to make clear from the start that any such communication with the therapist is to be open to both parties. In this way the therapist does not keep secrets for either partner and the point is made that open access to relevant information is desirable for all three parties concerned in this delicate process.

The rationale behind this ethical principle lies in the importance for the therapist of remaining clear and uncontaminated in his interactions with the couple's system. He needs to observe and work with these two people as they present themselves to him as a system. Any extraneous information he receives relating to the couple's process that he is prevented from sharing in the joint sessions by confidentiality imposed on him by one partner will render his task of remaining clear and open with them difficult, if not impossible. For example, if he has privately received the information from one partner that that person wishes to end the relationship but does not yet want to tell the other for fear of a strong reaction, then he will be placed in a position where he is 'pretending' to promote a process of reconciliation when he possesses secret information that this is not desired by both partners. Such therapy would simply be a charade and this example supports our concern about a firm adherence to this point of ethical practice.

SETTING CLEAR BOUNDARIES

The therapist will set a time boundary for each session and clearly contract for the total number of sessions. Since the therapy is brief-term, the end needs to be kept in view throughout the process so that all parties concerned are fully aware at any point of the number of sessions completed, and therefore of the number remaining to complete the work. The authors recommend that the couples therapist is not also in any other therapeutic relationship (individual or group) with either partner, and is therefore solely the therapist to the couple's relationship. The reasons informing this choice have already been touched upon in point 1 above. We consider that it is extremely difficult to maintain objectivity and therapeutic neutrality where the therapist has a prior or dual relationship with either partner. 'I don't suppose she has told you in her individual session that she isn't . . .'

would lead to the very splitting that can undermine the couples therapy. We prefer not to see either of the two people separately even initially for assessment purposes (as is sometimes done) because of the potential for projection where all information given the therapist is not done jointly. We are aware that we may differ from other practitioners in maintaining this position which has grown out of our and others' experience of precisely the kind of difficulty referred to here. Our practice has supported the view that a separate therapist for the couple (even if they are in group or individual therapy elsewhere) works in their best interests.

MAINTAINING BOUNDARIES OUTSIDE OF SESSIONS

It is of crucial importance that the therapist does not engage with either partner in discussions in between sessions which would have a systemic impact on the brief-term intervention as a whole, whilst also compromising the role of the therapist in the eyes of the other partner. So we recommend that any communications between sessions be confined to discussions about changes of appointment times and such administrative details should necessity demand this. In this instance, the ethical principle is very closely related to good practice.

Equally important is the issue of contracting carefully with the partners about their discussion of the therapy sessions in other contexts. Naturally they will refer to what has transpired and work with one another on mutual contracts between sessions. However, we have known cases where the in-session contact has become the subject of party chatter and banter, or where it is used manipulatively by either partner to coerce the other into agreement with their own point of view. 'He pretends here that he really wants to work on our relationship, but you should only know what fights we have been having about what I said to him in our last session here . . . .' Here we would recommend a caring agreement about how the process is used and what material is confidential to the couple *per se*. We see this as part of nourishing and protecting the relationship between these particular people. Where partners are in therapy individually or in a group simultaneously with the couples work, the extent to which details of the couples work are discussed in other therapeutic contexts will be the subject of careful negotiation. We are aware that some couples therapists will not engage with a couple if they are concurrently in therapy individually, but we have not found this an essential consideration. However, in such cases careful liaison with the other professionals involved, both before undertaking the therapy and in the course of it, is an essential component of good practice. Such consultation will operate in the best interests of both the clients, and will keep other professionals involved in their treatment informed about the process.

THERAPEUTIC NEUTRALITY

In couples work the issue of neutrality is crucial for the therapist where there are likely to be frequent invitations to take sides and favour one person's perspective over the other. Essential to a successful resolution is that you as therapist do not become part of the problem. As soon as you sense that you are beginning to favour one person's perspective over the other and ceasing to see the issue as a systemic one, then it is time to stop, take stock and get supervisory help. Sometimes as a therapist you may have a blind spot concerning a particular value because you regard it as universally accepted and do not question its applicability. For example, a therapist may not question the universal value of assertiveness as popularly defined, and therefore subtly impose this priority on the relationship not taking into account differing cultural norms in this regard. To guard against such an eventuality, supervision and consultation is essential to good practice. When we speak of neutrality, we are not implying that the therapist remain disengaged and distant from the members of the couple. We are referring more to an attitude of mind, to the therapeutic stance that the therapist takes in relation to the couple. It is vital that the therapist operate as the facilitator of a healthy process between the partners and does not herself become triangulated into the system and so undermine the value and the goals of the therapy. We are the first to acknowledge the challenge of maintaining this position of therapeutic neutrality whilst at the same time encountering the couple in a genuine, congruent and empathic manner. In an integrative approach, based on the centrality of relationship, it is important for the therapist to model for the couple open, empathic and genuine relating, whilst at the same time keeping in focus the agreed goals of the work. Where the therapist has reason to believe that his own needs, feelings or attitudes may be affecting the therapy adversely, he is ethically obliged to remedy this situation immediately with the aid of personal reflection and supervision.

COLLABORATING WITH OTHER PROFESSIONALS

In brief-term work with couples it is highly likely that you will be working in collaboration with other professionals. It may be that either or both partners are in individual therapy, or that you need to liaise with a GP or a psychiatrist, or with social services, where the welfare and safety of children is involved. In any of these events the nature of your reporting to other professionals needs to be clarified with the couple so that the boundaries of the therapeutic space are clear to them. If either partner is involved in other therapeutic work (individual or group) professionalism requires that the couples therapist contact these other practitioners and inform them of the couples therapy envisaged. A potential conflict may arise from competing goals in the different therapeutic contexts. For example, in an individual setting a therapist may support the expression of anger, which may then be acted out in relation to the other partner without the individual therapist's awareness of ill-advised timing or the complex systemic nature of the problem that evokes the angry response in one partner. We cannot rule out the possibility too, that whatever the avowed intention of the individual, the individual therapist may receive a biased account of a situation.

Any reporting about the process or content of the therapy must be discussed with the couple concerned and their agreement given to this. In addition to the issue of professional courtesy, we maintain that the support of all the professionals involved is more likely to ensure a successful outcome for the brief-term therapy with the couple.

LIMITS OF COMPETENCE

As in any therapeutic work, it is important to recognize the limits of your competence and make a further referral if necessary. On occasion, a referral to a sex therapist who specializes in the area of sexual problems may be required. Sometimes it may be more appropriate for the couple to be in long term couples work, or for the whole family to enter family therapy, or for the individual partners to engage in individual therapy or for one person to receive specialized help such as supplied by outplacement counselling. In some cases a medical or psychiatric intervention may be more appropriate, for example where one person is so severely depressed that he is unable to function and medical intervention becomes essential. With a client suffering from severe fragmentation of the self, long-term individual work may need to precede a couples intervention.

The therapist will need to take into account her own training and experience when taking on a couple for therapy. If this has not prepared her to work effectively with a particular couple (e.g. a gay male couple) then she is advised to make an appropriate referral to another practitioner experienced in this field. This means that the therapist is advised to have available a list of referral sources and directories to which she can refer the couple if she herself is not qualified to undertake the therapy. If a therapist is in doubt about his own ability or suitability for working with a couple, the supervisor can provide a sounding board for assessing the level of his competence in relation to the particular case.

THE LEGITIMATE USE OF POWER

The therapeutic relationship is a power-based relationship because of the power and authority vested in the therapist both by society and by his professional status and training. We consider the careful use of this legitimate power in the interests of the client/s to be a central ethical responsibility of any therapist practising in the field. For the brief-term couples therapist this is as central a consideration as it is in any other form of therapy. The couple approaching you are doing so because they trust that you will act in their best interests and will not in any way misuse or abuse the authority they invest in you because of your professional standing. Denying the power-base of the therapeutic relationship may lead the therapist to assume a kind of 'false equality' with clients ('we are all in this together') which discounts the responsibility and the special training that he brings to the interaction. The couple is consulting a person regarded as an expert in a field because they wish to benefit by this expertise and are paying the therapist for his professional skills in the service of their relationship. Any tendency to minimize this obvious inequality in experience, training and professional neutrality in relation to the proposed therapy will do the therapeutic work a disservice. We operate in a climate in which therapist abuse of power is in constant focus, sadly for the profession, and it behoves us as couples therapists not to add to the growing body of examples of unethical practice.

RESPECT AND COMMITMENT

A respect and commitment to relationship seems to us a prerequisite to working with couples. We work from an intersubjective perspective which acknowledges the need for bonding in relationship as a primary motivational factor in human beings. The therapist provides a model of relationship to the couple that is reparative in its own right, whilst also facilitating the development of a rewarding relationship between them as partners. It is important for the couples therapist to maintain an I–Thou stance in relation to clients, to aim to be present for them and respect their attempts to reach one another (Buber, 1994). Compassion for people struggling to reach one another, to understand and be understood, forms a good basis for effective brief-term work. The practice of inclusion (Buber 1994; Yontef 1993; Hycner, 1993) is an important component in the therapist's capacity to appreciate the frames of reference and the subjective experience of both partners.

The therapist will be particularly challenged in brief-term therapy to engage fully, intervene cleanly and then let go elegantly. This constant process of engagement and disengagement requires discipline, a certain therapeutic asceticism and regular supervisory support for this highly demanding type of work.

RESPECT FOR DIVERSITY

A non-judgemental and open frame of mind in relation to frames of reference different from the therapist's own is critical to the success of brief therapy with couples. It is important that the therapist does not impose his own models of relationship on others. There are many different and satisfying ways of being a couple, all of which may possess their own unique features that do not necessarily relate directly to the dimensions outlined in this book. An individual couple needs to find its own balance within the relationship parameters of relevance to them. The task of the brief-couples therapist is to facilitate this process. Some people have three-way relationships of long standing in our culture, a mode of relating that is frowned upon by prevailing norms. One of the authors was once involved in counselling such a threesome, taking into account the diverse needs of the individuals and the needs of the children brought together in this way. Lesbian couples may prefer a way of relating that involves living on one's own and engaging in a relationship or relationships of choice, at a level comfortable to the individual. The added challenge of working with cross-cultural or interracial couples may further take issue with many of the assumptions we hold dear in western cultures. It is important for the brief-term couples therapist to be available to a diversity and range of partnerships, which may cross racial, cultural, religious, educational and class divides.

12

CASE STUDY

It is our intention in this chapter to present a case study of a brief-term intervention with a couple which illustrates the approach that we have outlined in this book. We have done this by means of a commentary on the process of the work, interspersed with excerpts from the sessions to give the reader a sense of the process that takes place. We have also included the *full assessment* of the couple in order to demonstrate how this is done and subsequently how this material is incorporated in the sessions. In summarizing material gleaned from the assessment session and the eight sessions following this, we trust that we have given the reader sufficient information for purposes of effective illustration.

INTRODUCING THE COUPLE

Jessica and Grant presented for treatment because Jessica was expressing difficulty in dealing with Morgan, Grant's 13-year-old son from a previous marriage. Grant was finding the situation increasingly stressful. Jessica was a 29-year-old social worker in a local authority, who married Grant two years previously. Jessica had one previous long-standing relationship which started when she was sixteen and still at school. This relationship lasted for a period of nine years with several break-ups. Since she had expected to marry this young man, she felt rootless and lacking in direction after the end of her first love relationship. This period culminated in a reactive depression. She subsequently threw herself into her career as a social worker and became very involved with the adolescents in her care. She rapidly gained the respect of her colleagues for her effective work with this age-group. This is her first marriage.

Grant was a 43-year old engineer with his own small engineering business. He was already divorced when Jessica met him at their local church. Grant in his turn had married his childhood love who was the girl next door and the same age as he was. They married at 21; they had the misfortune that their first two babies miscarried so that when Morgan was born his arrival was accompanied both by anxiety and by great excitement. By the time they were in their thirties beginning to move out of the early symbiotic phase of their relationship, both Grant and his wife Melody realized that their initial attraction had not survived the stress of the last ten years of pain and disillusionment. The divorce involved tension and acrimony, particularly around custody and access to Morgan. Subsequent to his divorce, Grant had several short-lived encounters, but when he met Jessica he immediately felt that he had at last 'found a soul-mate', someone who could truly understand and provide him with the support and companionship that he longed for in a union.

The tension in Jessica and Grant's relationship arose from Grant's expectations of how Jessica would be a substitute mother to Morgan. The difficulty for Jessica was that not having her own child, she suddenly found herself required to be a parent to a 13-year old who had his own mother. This expectation was exacerbated by her failure to fall pregnant in contrast to her heartfelt desire to have her own child by Grant. Her tension around falling pregnant evoked for Grant many of the feelings previously involved in the traumas of his earlier experiences of miscarriages with his first wife, Melody. Jessica and Grant consulted their local vicar who had known them both since childhood and whose judgement they respected.

The immediate presenting issue at the assessment session appeared to be the frequency of Morgan's visits to the household. He lived a few streets away with his mother who was part of the same community. As his mother had a job involving regular business trips, he often stayed with Jessica and Grant at short notice. Jessica felt 'intruded upon' by this, whereas Grant was happy 'to give his son a home' in this way. Morgan also spent the school holidays with Jessica and Grant.

When Jessica's 'childhood' relationship ended she had gone to a counsellor for some sessions because she had felt that she was 'falling apart' at the time and was becoming progressively more depressed. The experience of counselling had been good for her; she had felt very helped by her sessions. Grant, on the other hand, had no previous experience of counselling or therapy. Although divorce mediation had been suggested at the time of the break-up of his marriage, he had resisted, believing that 'one should be able to manage one's own problems'. As Jessica became more and more desperate, she became afraid that she might sink into a similar depression to the one that she had previously experienced. Finally, succumbing not only to her urgency, but out of his very real concern for her wellbeing, Grant agreed to go with her to the local vicar. The vicar, who had known them both from childhood and was concerned about their welfare as he recognized the growing tensions in their relationship, felt relieved when they finally arrived on his doorstep. He had seen some good results arising out of the work that the brief-term therapist at a local health centre offered and had an intuitive sense himself that they would be a good couple for this approach.

BACKGROUND INFORMATION

In the course of the initial (assessment) session, the therapist gathered the following background information about the couple. Jessica's early childhood had been stable and 'normal' in the usual middle-class sense of an earlier generation, although her grandparents (on both sides) had had to deal with the challenge of moving to England from Jamaica. Her parents remained married to each other, father working and mother staying at home to raise the children. Jessica was the oldest child in her family. When she was born both parents were a little disappointed that their first child was a girl. However, they apparently became reconciled to her gender and each developed their own expectations of her. In fact Jessica remembers her mother saying to her as a little girl: 'I'm so pleased to have a daughter, because you are going to be mummy's little helper!'

This was particularly reiterated when the other two children were born. There is quite a large age difference between Jessica and her siblings. Her first brother was born when she was five years old and just about ready for school. She experienced his birth as a big shock. Her parents and grandparents made a big fuss over this baby, who was not only the first son, but also the first grandson on both sides. She undoubtedly felt displaced and was often physically ill during the first year of her brother's life. Starting school slightly younger than her peers did not help the unnoticed stress she experienced as a young child who suddenly felt pressured to grow up. She particularly felt the loss of her father's attention. Three years later another brother was born with a congenital heart defect, so that Jessica was often burdened with the additional responsibility of looking after her first brother, who was an active, mischievous and boisterous child. She frequently experienced herself as being blamed for his 'naughtiness'. As some of the history emerged, the therapist thought that it was likely that being expected to look after Morgan may well trigger some of her repressed and unremembered childhood anxiety about being held responsible for her brother's behaviour.

Grant in many ways reminded Jessica of her father. In the early stages of their relationship, while they were courting, she may unconsciously have re-experienced being at the centre of attention and feeling unique and special, much the way she had as a very young child, before the advent of her siblings. When they married and Morgan's place in Grant's life became a reality for her she again re-experienced the early and painful displacement. The attraction to Grant and the unconscious hope that she would finally have her father's sole attention and be the preferred and special child was constantly threatened by Morgan. Inevitably he represented the younger, and in her experience, the more attractive rivals for attention.

Grant was the second son in a family of four. His oldest brother attracted both the advantages and disadvantages of being the oldest son. After Grant's arrival, a third son was born and then lastly a baby sister. Grant, sandwiched in between, somehow lived his childhood without too much pressure but also without too much attention, in a fairly strict authoritarian family. He did to a degree feel that he was overlooked with the bulk of the attention going to his older brother or to the one girl in the family. His sister seemed to get away with a lot of things, especially avoiding the duties and expectations of performance that were laid on the boys in this family.

Grant's first marriage was a psychological move to leave home and escape, while at the same time get some of the special attention and love that had been missing in his childhood. When that marriage failed he was left with a lot of unexpressed sadness and anger. He had not dealt with any of these feelings or the other stresses in his marriage at the time of his divorce so that he carried this legacy into his relationship with Jessica. In meeting Jessica and feeling that he had found a 'soul mate' it was as though he too, had discovered the person who would value and love him and really see him for himself. On the one hand he could not really understand or empathize with Jessica's problem with Morgan; however, on the other hand at an emotional level she reminded him of his younger sister and younger brother who continually seemed to be competing for his attention and approval. The tension it aroused in him caused him to want to shut down and withdraw emotionally as it left him somewhat helpless and exhausted.

INITIAL ASSESSMENT SESSION

At the initial assessment, Jessica and Grant were clear about their shared desire for help with Morgan. Underlying this presenting problem, their repressed anger and resentment towards each other was clear to the therapist, although these feelings only gradually became overt in the course of the sessions.

In the assessment session Jessica and Grant started off by talking in a very reasonable fashion about the impact of Morgan's unscheduled visits to their home. Jessica presented her observations in the manner of a case conference delivery, without displaying any obvious signs of emotion. Grant was more overtly distressed and provocative in his comments about Jessica's inability to 'relate normally to Morgan'. It was clear at this stage that they had very different ideas about child-rearing though this awareness was not further elaborated between them.

An excerpt from the preliminary assessment session illustrates their interlocking non-productive cycle of interaction. Grant accused Jessica of being over-solicitous and preoccupied by Morgan's personal hygiene whilst ignoring his son's need for affection and his yearning for her interest in his world. A short sample from this discussion illustrates the process that is outlined in Figure 4.

JESSICA: I've tried to be like a good mother to Morgan. I know things have not been easy for him. Perhaps you (the therapist) can explain to me why he is so angry with me? He appreciates nothing I do for him, even though I'm often tidying up after him and buying the food he enjoys.

GRANT: I can tell you what the matter is – you are plain stupid to fuss over him all the time. You ought to realize that 13 year olds are quite

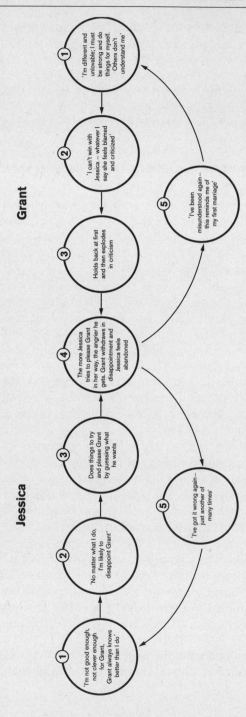

Figure 4: Jessica and Grant's reinforcing cycle of non-communication (based on Goldfried (1985), with permission)

capable of looking after themselves. You demand too little responsibility of a child of his age. Why not spend your energy talking to
him instead of babying him?

JESSICA: You're so critical of me. I feel constantly in the wrong. I know
you really don't respect me. I was afraid from the start that I would
not be intelligent enough as a wife for you.

GRANT: That's where I always get caught. If I tell you what I think,
you accuse me of criticizing you. If I keep quiet, then I'm not supporting you. A guy can't win with you.

This dialogue illustrates how easily and readily the couple used the
issue of Morgan and consciously experienced this problem as the focus
of differences. Although they felt that they started out rationally the
discussion rapidly turned into an argument. The anger and blaming
triggered each partner's belief system. Jessica felt criticized and at
fault, believing that she was 'not good enough' a support or helper. For
Grant the criticism felt as though he could not win. He found this
situation reminiscent of his first marriage, in which constant nagging
and blaming left him feeling double-bound and angry: 'I'm damned if I
do, and I'm damned if I don't!'

Information gleaned from both the initial session and the beginning
phase of the therapy yielded a picture of the interlocking 'vicious cycle'
of non-communication in Jessica and Grant's relationship.

In this initial assessment session, the therapist allowed the dialogue
and the quarrel to continue for a while, in order to get a sense of their
underlying belief systems and particularly how their core interpersonal schemata interlock and reinforce one another.

Couples will inevitably wait for a session in order to have a fight with
the therapist present. Each of them is hoping for affirmation and confirmation of their position. At another level they are also hoping finally
to be able to find help or resolve the the situation. The hope of finding
help is an important unconscious motive that brings people into
therapy. The therapist sees their unconsciously driven need to start
fighting early on in the treatment as a helpful and positive sign.

For this couple however, the therapist did understand that the management of Morgan needed to be addressed, while at the same time the way

they expressed their difficulties pointed to the underlying dynamics and earlier unresolved issues that each brought to this relationship.

In summary then, the therapist was hearing and listening for the manifest problem, whilst noting indications of their earlier relationship experiences and aspects of their developmental histories that were surfacing in their current lives. He registered the nature and process of their reinforcing cycle of non-problem-solving interactions for future intervention.

ASSESSMENT BY THE THERAPIST OF JESSICA AND GRANT

The following assessment of Jessica and Grant's relationship dimensions emerged from the assessment session and provided the basis for goal-setting and contracting.

Compatibility of Value Systems and Frames of Reference

Jessica and Grant had a considerable degree of compatibility and shared familiarity of concerns, coming from the same parish and a similar educational background. Although the manifest conflict was in relation to child-rearing, there is a basic agreement about priorities in life. However, the disagreement they expressed about handling the child reflected the differing loyalties that resulted from the fact that this was a second marriage for Grant, while Jessica was coming in to a pre-formed relationship between father and son.

The experience of being a parent profoundly affects and influences adult experience. Until one has a child or begins parenting a child in the ordinary course of adult life, there is little need to deal with or remember one's own experiences of being parented in childhood. However, one's emotional and intuitive responses as a parent are powerfully influenced by one's own early experience. In Jessica and Grant's case, he has had the experience of parenting from when Morgan was born. In fact, when Morgan was little Grant often took over the major task of caring for him, including waking up at night and looking after him when he was ill. Jessica, on the other hand largely operated from her theoretical ideas, having had no experiential basis for rearing a child. She considered herself 'good with adolescents' since she managed her cases well. However, there is a vast difference in client management which is time-limited and well-boundaried and translating that into family life which in this case involved forming a relationship with a somewhat complicated only child who had already experienced a split home and a good deal of loss at a young age.

Effectiveness of Problem-solving and Conflict Resolution

Jessica and Grant dealt effectively with the day-to-day running of their lives and could resolve practical problems with speed and efficiency. The therapist assessed them as being effective in this dimension, which is a good indicator for brief-term work.

However, their problem-solving in this instance was undermined by the lack of recognition of the impact of pre-existing loyalties, of the traumatic effects of previous miscarriages and of Jessica and Grant's frustrated desire for a child from their union. These unrecognized emotions interfered with their customary ability to resolve problems.

Emotional issues and previous early experience interfere with the problem-solving abilities of normal effective adults. When adults cannot use their problem-solving skills it is a good indication that emotional factors play a part. In Jessica and Grant's case, there was the painful and frustrating situation of her difficulty in conceiving a baby coupled with her longing for a child of her own. Both Jessica and Grant's response to solving this problem was affected by their positions and experience in their families of origin.

Emotional Intimacy, Capacity to Have Fun and to Achieve Sexual Gratification

The mutual attraction and capacity to enjoy one another that originally brought Jessica and Grant together was rapidly being eroded by the tensions and stress of their differences concerning Morgan and their unexpressed disappointment about their own desired baby. The therapist's assessment of this dimension however confirmed a basic capacity for intimacy and a mutually fulfilling sexual and gratifying marriage.

Often this capacity is difficult to assess, since couples come into therapy anxious and angry and with a determination to show the worst and malfunctioning aspects of their relationship to the therapist. The therapist needs to ask direct questions like: 'How do you enjoy yourselves? What do you do for fun? What first attracted you to each other? What would you like more of in your lives?' In Jessica and Grant's case it quickly became clear that they did have the capacity to enjoy each other and themselves together.

It is also necessary to ask directly about the couple's sexual relationship, which we see as a barometer of the marriage. In making an assessment the therapist needs to ask direct questions. It is pointless in this brief-term approach to wait for one of the couple to drop in information like 'there has been no sex between us in the past six months'; the therapist needs to enquire about this in the assessment phase. Sexual attraction in modern marriages usually underlies the basis for 'falling in love'. However, it can rapidly and easily become eroded in the face of anger and anxiety. An initial compatibility and attraction is a good prognostic indicator of a vibrancy and capacity to enjoy each other and have fun together. Having our sexuality affirmed, valued and appreciated affirms us at our deepest level of being. In Jessica and Grant's case the aim is that the therapeutic intervention will assist in clearing away the aspects eroding their relationship and allow for the restoration of their fundamental mutual attraction for each other to blossom.

In this case, in fact, the relationship is far better sexually than their previous ones had been. The therapist feels encouraged by this and reassured that there are strong ties that hold them together. The need for sex therapy would bring in its wake the possibility of the need for further intervention. It was with relief therefore that the therapist felt reassured on this dimension of their relationship.

Caring for the Other, Giving Support, Warmth and Succour in Times of Need

Jessica and Grant showed a high degree of mutual caring and support indicating a strong bond between them. The therapist concluded that this was a good prognostic indicator for the successful future of their relationship since they experienced good will, love and concern for the other's well-being.

This was a particularly strong aspect of Jessica and Grant's relationship. Despite some of their childhood disappointments and experiences in previous love affairs, they both came from fundamentally reliable and stable situations, in which they experienced sufficient care and concern allowing them to be responsible caring adults. As we have already indicated, if this dimension is lacking in one or both partners, we would see this as a serious level of disturbance and think that long-term work would be indicated. It may be necessary to support a partner to leave a relationship when the other partner is seriously deficient on this dimension, as in cases of violence and abuse.

Assessing the Level of Awareness of the 'Problem' as Experienced by Self and Other

Jessica and Grant agreed that there was a problem between them which they tended to focus on their different approaches to dealing with Morgan. However, they were only dimly aware of the significant emotional areas in their relationship that were unspoken, stressful influences between them arising from their frustration and disappointment about the desire for a baby and Grant's prior pain related to his first wife's miscarriages. In addition, they had not sufficiently accounted for the impact on their relationship of Grant's pre-existing bond with his son and the requirements and implications of this connection. Therefore, the therapist decided on an initial focus to bring to their awareness these underlying issues in order to come to some agreed formulation of the problem.

At the deeper level, of course, their early family life and developmental history also affected the here and now perception of the problem. However, the therapist decided on an initial focus on current interactions. In this case the manifest issues were very clear and it was also clear that there was 'unfinished business' in relation to them. The therapist knows that working with the unexpressed feelings is both important and immediately beneficial. As people get in touch with their unexpressed emotions, the connections, irrational beliefs and repressed memories emerge, allowing them to understand and recognize how they are trying to deal with and make sense of their feelings.

Developmental Assessment

Normalizing the phases of change in relationships by describing the developmental process is a useful intervention. Couples often experience a sense of relief at the explanation and understanding that this brings them. The fact that others have been there before and that their experience of confusion and anxiety can be explained and understood is very important and relieves some of the worry 'that there is something wrong with them'. The therapist observes that Jessica and Grant appear to be moving from the symbiotic–symbiotic phase into the differentiating process. This provides a useful point of intervention. Effective change at this point can avert a move into a hostile–dependent phase by creating the basis for open clear communication, tolerance of difference and the development of good coping mechanisms to deal with emotionally laden issues. It was in this area that Grant's previous marriage foundered. The therapist will confront the early signs of hostile–dependence and facilitate emotional sharing.

SUITABILITY FOR AND CONSIDERATION OF CONTRAINDICATIONS FOR BRIEF-TERM THERAPY

Their suitability for brief-term work was based on the following: their joint identification of the problem as a difference about parenting values, strategies and personal boundaries; their stated commitment to use the help of the therapist; and their ability to understand and articulate the issues and accept the psychological conceptualization of their presenting conflict. It also appeared as if they had good clear ego functioning and although there were difficulties now, neither of them seemed to suffer from deep-seated and longstanding personality problems. However, the presenting issues reflected some of their inherent differences and difficulties in relationship and in negotiating intimate contact, a legacy from their childhood experiences and subsequent unsuccessful relationships.

A strong indication of their suitability for brief therapy was the lack of severe pathology in either Jessica or Grant. Jessica and Grant presented as basically well functioning and well meaning. Both were invested in a long-term future. Their histories and external stresses had led to a breakdown in their normal coping mechanisms and ability to deal with conflict. The resurgence of old unproductive patterns of interaction complicated the current situation. They shared an assumption that differences of opinion imply a lack of love: 'If you loved me, you wouldn't disagree with me.' Although Grant was the one who most frequently gave voice to this belief, Jessica complied with it by according him the authority to be right or wrong.

Clearly Jessica and Grant did not suffer from severe disorders such as those referred to at the end of Chapter 4. They both had the good fortune to grow up in intact families with normal parents suffering from the ordinary difficulties of childhood. What complicated their lives right now was the child from a previous marriage and how that stress intersects with the past. The severe problems mentioned at the conclusion to the chapter on assessment arose from trauma, deficit and neglect. Psychological problems in parents usually persist and are carried over into the next generation if there is no intervention. Thus Morgan as a child of a broken home became a child at risk, although he would not necessarily have problems if his situation was accounted for and addressed by Grant and Jessica. Grant was the first person in his family to get divorced and initially his divorce was met with distress and disapproval by his parents. His ex-wife, Melody, had a close relationship with his mother and she in turn missed her previous daughter-in-law. Consequently she had difficulty in accepting Jessica. Although capable of creating much hurt and pain, family problems of this nature are more easily dealt with and resolved by recognition and talking, than the ones described in our discussion of contraindications.

The overall assessment by the therapist confirmed therefore that there are no apparent contraindications for brief-term work with Jessica and Grant. The therapist agreed to see Jessica and Grant for eight sessions (subsequent to the assessment) with a review built into the sixth session and with the possibility of further series of sessions in 6–8 months time. The therapist explained his role to the couple as a facilitator of the process and not as a 'judge' or 'referee'.

In the subsequent section, we will give a flavour of the work with this couple. This will take the form of brief excerpts from each of the eight sessions interspersed with a commentary. Inevitably the reader will need to extrapolate from what is given to fill in the story. We trust we have given sufficient material to give a sense of the likely sequence in a brief intervention of this type.

SESSION I: AGREEING THE THERAPEUTIC CONTRACT

In the first session of the brief-term therapy, Grant and Jessica were each bursting to give their own version of recent events, cherishing the illusion and the hope that the therapist will clearly 'recognize' that 'I am right in the way I see things' and at last someone will validate 'my way of understanding the issues'.

In response to the therapist's invitation for them to give their description of the presenting issue as they see it, Jessica started and was soon interrupted by Grant. They continued by interrupting each other, talking over one another – each in their eagerness to put their case to the therapist. The therapist allowed the process to proceed for a while before intervening. By this time the couple were beginning to escalate their level of argument, their voices getting louder, and there was a sense of desperation on both sides.

THERAPIST: I appreciate that you both feel very passionately about this issue. And I notice that in your eagerness to give your own point of view you often cut the other person off short.

(Both Grant and Jessica paused at this point and the session continues as follows:)

JESSICA: You're right. I think we are both so excitable that there are times when neither of us stops to listen to the other one.

GRANT: It would be quite simple if you would give me my say without contradicting me all the time.

JESSICA: It's amazing how whenever we are trying to sort something out, you always manage to make it my fault. If you could stop being so critical of me, I might stop contradicting you.

THERAPIST: Let's pause there for a moment so that we can check out what each of you is feeling at this point.

The therapist turned to Grant and then to Jessica. (In turning to one member of the couple, the task for the therapist is to make it clear that he/she is not taking sides.)

An exploration of both their feeling states revealed that each of them was feeling misunderstood and disregarded by the other. The therapist proceeded to encourage each person to speak and the other to reflect back what they heard so that Grant and Jessica could listen and be heard. They could begin to experience that they would be given a chance to have their say and could therefore stop and listen to the other.

THERAPIST: Jessica, what are you feeling right now?

JESSICA: Angry and hurt and attacked.

THERAPIST: And you Grant? What is going on for you?

GRANT: I'm angry and I feel misunderstood.

THERAPIST: What else?

GRANT: I guess I feel sad as well because this feels so familiar to me and we keep going round and round and I know it will only end in anger and frustration.

(The therapist felt encouraged that Jessica and Grant so readily acknowledged and expressed their feelings and that they were willing to be this open in an early phase in the treatment. Some time later in the session, Jessica and Grant began another of their familiar fights, again with a view to get help, albeit indirectly.)

GRANT: And another thing – you always arrive home exhausted and preoccupied with your clients and never seem to notice that anything else is going on.

(There the therapist intervened before Jessica had a chance to come back with one of her customary defensive, although subtly attacking, comments).

THERAPIST: Grant, can you be more specific about what you feel when Jessica comes home tired and preoccupied?

(The idea here was to undercut the blaming and go for a clear 'I' statement. The therapist also noted the use of 'always', 'never' and other exaggerated over-inclusive language but decided to leave this unconfronted for the time being.)

The therapist's goal in this first session was to focus on the communication and to create a therapeutic culture in which each partner respected the other's right to speak their mind and be heard. In this way the therapist provided a more creative process for interaction that can be transferred beyond the therapeutic context.

By the end of the first session, the working contract between Jessica, Grant and the therapist was clearly formulated.

The therapeutic contract arrived at with Jessica and Grant can be summarized as follows:

- to focus on the way they both related to Morgan in order to find a satisfactory and mutually agreed course of action;
- to manage the stress they were experiencing in their desire to have a baby and communicate their feelings without damaging each other in the process.

They agreed that in this process they needed to explore the differences between them in order to resolve their current conflict.

The relationship between the contract and the therapeutic aims and goals can be seen as follows. The therapist was proceeding on the hypothesis that these two people were having difficulty in accepting and respecting each other's different beliefs and frames of references, as manifested principally in the child-rearing issue. The therapist therefore anticipated that their work would start with the incompatibilities of their frames of reference in this regard, but might very well soon move to exploration of unexpressed and unacknowledged fears, disappointments and expectations of the other. He also anticipated that he might need to do some work with them on the impact of Grant's previous marital experience on their newly constituted home.

The therapist's goal included the provision of a safe context for the partners to raise to their awareness the underlying, unexplored feelings and memories that interfered with their ability to negotiate successfully on the practical issues related to Morgan. The therapist would be alert to any interlocking and dysfunctional communication patterns that each partner brought to the current process. In addition to the educative aspects of the therapy, there was also the opportunity for healing and resolving previous painful experiences. An optimal outcome of this process would enable the partners to move forward with each other more fully in the present without the 'baggage' from the past confounding current concerns.

The contracting phase started off on a useful footing despite their initial disagreements at the outset of the first session. Jessica and Grant were clear about their commitment to each other and to the marriage. They were also committed to working out their differences and making this marriage work. They each felt sure of their own need and wish for a long-term enduring monogamous partnership and considered that the other provided them with a good compatible choice. The therapist concluded that being able to formulate a contract as clearly as they had is helpful to the work between them all. Most people in our society do not have very good skills at expressing or negotiating conflict. As these skills can be learnt, therapy and counselling are particularly helpful in this regard.

SESSION 2: WORKING THROUGH THE ISSUE OF COMPATIBILITY OF VALUE SYSTEMS AND FRAMES OF REFERENCE

In the second session, the main theme centred around the concern that diversity and difference does not equate with a lack of love, care and respect. Jessica and Grant introduced their concern about Morgan's impending visit over the summer holidays, and how they were going to provide enough opportunity for fun and excitement for a 13-year-old without disrupting their adult lives, and driving a wedge between. They had unfortunate memories of the alienation and conflict that followed a previous visit that took them months to recover from and restore their equilibrium. It became clear through their discussion of how to arrange the activities and adequate child care, that they had no efficient way of dealing with disagreements and negotiating a satisfactory resolution to this emotionally laden conflict. The therapist was intervening in their discussion, particularly as Grant seemed to be laying down the law and making unilateral demands of Jessica without

negotiation. Grant feels irritated and frustrated at the continual inter-
ruptions by the therapist and what he perceives as criticisms. The
therapist, recognizing his irritation, pauses and checks it out with him.

THERAPIST: Grant, it seems as if you feel criticised by my last comment?

(Here the therapist is modelling a direct way of picking up and dealing
with underlying feelings without getting critical or hostile. Also he is
showing empathy and sensitivity to the impact he makes on Grant.
Grant readily responds to his invitation while Jessica carefully observes this process.)

GRANT: Yes, actually I do. It seems as if whatever Jessica says you
support or agree with, whereas you make me feel wrong and difficult.

This was a crucial point in the brief therapy as the couple are inevitably
going to attempt to triangulate the therapist into their process. The
very nature of such an invitation was inherent in this dynamic configuration, with its Oedipal possibilities. Each partner would compete to
be right while at the same time seeing the therapist as more likely to
favour or support the other. As we have explained, it is important for
the therapist not only to explain but also to make clear that he is not in
the business of taking sides or favouring one person over the other. In
this instance the therapist was not even feeling particularly supportive
of Jessica and so could easily recognize the projection on Grant's part.
The therapist now has a choice of going further and exploring why a
request for clarification was experienced as a criticism or continuing to
help the couple clarify the communication. The therapist decided in
this case to stay with the couple's communication, making a mental
note however to deal more directly with Grant's internal organizing
matrix if it kept interfering with their direct contact and if it blocked
the communication between the couple. At this stage he confined himself to a simple clarifying question.

THERAPIST: What do you need me to know that I may be misunderstanding about your position?

(This gave Grant the opportunity to voice his feelings and the therapist
could then proceed with unravelling the communication between the
couple. The therapist continued to explore their attitudes to Morgan's
visits.)

GRANT: I think you should make sure that you are around for Morgan; perhaps take off a few days from work to be around for him and his friends. They need a mother around to give support and understanding; perhaps be something of a friend.

JESSICA: He is arriving just when I have to go to court in that child abuse case, so it won't be possible for me to take the time off. You do it instead. Anyway he is not a social work case of mine, so I don't have the influence over him that you seem to be assuming I have.

GRANT: You have me totally confused now. You won't take time off to be with Morgan during his holiday, yet during term-time when he comes around, you never leave him in peace. I think your nagging him about meals and bathing just aggravates the situation. ·

JESSICA (turning to therapist): You see I can never win – whatever I do for Morgan I don't get it right for Grant. I can't be the mother he wants for his son.

THERAPIST (addressing Grant): In asking Jessica to take time off from work, what are you hoping for in her relationship with Morgan?

GRANT: I was hoping that Jessica could become a friend to Morgan . . . someone he can chat to about school and his struggles . . . and that she could help him adjust.

JESSICA: Look Morgan is not one of my clients and I don't want to take him on as a case!

GRANT: I'm not asking for that . . . why not just be normal and friendly as you are to me and others?

JESSICA: But Morgan isn't friendly to me and resents it when I ask him to do things.

THERAPIST: I understand from what you say, Grant, that you are hoping that Jessica and Morgan can be friends.

GRANT: Yes, and I'm really scared that Morgan's presence may come between me and Jessica.

JESSICA: I'm also scared . . . perhaps if we both know about each other's fears . . . that will help.

(In this way, the therapist begins to bring to the surface the unspoken wishes and underlying assumptions that are influencing their attitudes to the problem.)

SESSION 3: A FOCUS ON PROBLEM-SOLVING

The therapist took the initiative in this session to focus on problem-solving techniques. Although Grant and Jessica were listening to one another, they were still experiencing considerable difficulty in respecting each other's unique perspective on the issue which had been evoked by Morgan's presence in the home. The therapist was aware that although the current content and focus was on Morgan, the deficit in problem-solving skills probably extended to other areas of Grant and Jessica's relationship.

Given the differing expectations each had of their own and the other's relationship with Morgan which had surfaced in session 2, Grant and Jessica had agreed to focus in session 3 on negotiating realistic agreements concerning Morgan. Jessica had arrived at an understanding of Grant's view of himself as a father and his definition of his duty and responsibility in that role. Grant in his turn appreciated that Jessica, not having children of her own, had no direct experience of parenting, despite the nature of her work.

THERAPIST: We agreed that we would start off today's session with a discussion about arrangements for Morgan's summer holidays. In doing this we need to focus on specific tasks and responsibilities that each of you will undertake.

GRANT: Before we do that, I want to make sure that you understand . . .

THERAPIST: I would like to hold you to our agreement. Are you willing to discuss the arrangements for Morgan or do you wish to negotiate a change of contract?

(Therapist stays focused on the agreed task, noting, however, Grant's resistance, which will need to be checked back on later.)

JESSICA: I have given this a lot of thought and what I suggest is that we have a sit-down discussion with Morgan on the first evening to find out what he wants to do during his break. That way he will be included in making the plans, rather than that we impose our agenda on him.

GRANT: That will be asking for trouble . . . you'll have requests for night clubs, visits to the covered ski slopes, trips to Brighton, tickets for gigs . . . I can just see it coming.

JESSICA: That is not what I meant to suggest at all. I simply want Morgan to share in an adult discussion of plans so that he feels included.

THERAPIST: If you do agree on such a meeting with Morgan, then not only Morgan but each of you as well can state your needs clearly.

Although both partners seemed rational and were able to agree logically that it was a matter of simply sitting down and discussing the issue, the therapist was aware that the underlying feelings were just below the surface and liable to emerge readily. Sure enough Grant began to 'Yes . . . but' every suggestion that Jessica made. In this instance the therapist went for a process decision rather than addressing the content of the quarrel. Couples have many topics to fight about – money, sex, in-laws, family holidays, friends etc. In therapy, identifying and exposing the underlying process of the fight circumvents having to deal with all the many contentious issues they could find as a focus for disagreement. The therapist pointed out the way Grant said 'Yes . . . but' to each suggestion of Jessica's while at the same time subtly redefining everything she says.

JESSICA: I really feel strongly about having a meeting that includes Morgan so that he can share in making plans.

GRANT: That sounds a good idea but you know how impossible it is to agree even where we should have a snack before a movie . . . I can't see this working.

JESSICA: I was trying to come up with a plan and you immediately disagree. I always feel put down by you, Grant.

GRANT: I don't put you down Jessica . . . you are so sensitive and take everything I say as a rejection or criticism.

Jessica: Well, I clearly am not good enough for you, Grant.

(The therapist, recognizing this as one of their familiar roundabouts, decided to nip this one in the bud.)

THERAPIST: Jessica, what do you mean by 'not good enough'?

JESSICA (tearfully and very much the victim now):   I mean he makes me feel awful.

THERAPIST: I'm not sure I understand how anyone makes someone else feel. What happens inside you Jessica when you experience Grant putting you down?

JESSICA: What happens is I start feeling little and scared and I remember how my brothers would tease me, mother was always criticizing me and blaming me and Dad would not even look up from his newspaper.

THERAPIST: So what happens next?

JESSICA: Well I feel just awful and believe that there's something really wrong with me.

(Therapist decides to bring this back to Grant and Jessica and not go into the early scenes now as it seems more useful to stay with the couples' communication at this juncture.)

THERAPIST: So Grant *always* (stresses the word) makes you feel small and inadequate?

JESSICA (able to recognise her part in the process):   I guess only when he's so uncommunicative.

This session then also became one that focused on clarifying communication, looking at underlying issues and confronting the couple's need to keep scoring points off each other. They had, however, by now relaxed considerably and felt more secure and trusting of the process.

They were also more able to catch themselves or each other at their favourite game and even become humorous at times in this process. Humour is a great source of energy and support in therapy. Where a therapist can use it, it is possible to confront or say difficult things elegantly and effectively. When clients become humorous again it is a good indication of their ability to gain a perspective on themselves and also be objective, while at the same time use the 'play space' provided by the therapeutic context.

GRANT (As he was about to set a trap to catch Jessica out on some contradiction in her account of events):   There I was just about to catch you Jessica and show you up again. I'm afraid its another of those family games that Dad was so good at. And I learnt it, although I always tried to duck and dive and avoid being caught out myself!

THERAPIST: Well done, Grant. That's a very important insight that you've just reached.

It is really important to underline partners' strengths and good points as well as confronting their unhelpful ones. Problem-solving is one of the strengths that this couple possess as well as quite a good degree of self-insight and awareness. The therapist reflecting on the session decides that it is important to go for the underlying and deeper issues in the next session. He feels that unless the embedded issues are exposed and addressed, they could continue to re-emerge and prevent a long-lasting result.

SESSION 4: RE-AFFIRMING INTIMACY

As the therapist listened to Jessica and Grant's negotiation about Morgan, he became aware that the couple had little time alone available for their relationship. The fun appears to have gone out of the picture while the arguments have centred around Morgan and their preoccupation with Jessica's possible pregnancy. Grant has clearly been giving thought to this issue.

GRANT: Since our last meeting (turns to the therapist) your words have stayed with me: 'When did the two of you last spend time together that was relaxing and enjoyable?' Frankly, I couldn't remember. We seem to spend most of our time working, arguing about Morgan or feeling stressed about Jessica not falling pregnant. I feel as though we are on a slippery downward slide.

JESSICA: Are you regretting that you married me? I know that I will never be as perfect a wife to you as your Mum was to your Dad, but I do try . . . and not falling pregnant upsets me as well.

GRANT: Jessica please, when are you going to believe that I love you for you; I am not expecting some perfect TV advertisement wife, but a real live companion and partner – problems and all.

JESSICA: I know you care about me Grant, but I don't understand how come I'm so often left feeling not good enough for you . . .

THERAPIST: Jessica, what usually precedes your feeling not good enough?

In this way, the therapist explored with Grant and Jessica the process that undermined their intimacy. As the therapist empathically asked Jessica this question, he noticed that she had become shaky and tearful, even as she struggled to avoid becoming 'over-emotional'. His empathy touched her and precipitated a burst of emotion. The words came tumbling out, and what emerged were her long-felt and unacknowledged feelings that her brothers were always more important, more valuable, more special, than she ever was. As a little girl she felt she could never be 'good enough' for her parents. As she gets in touch with these early memories of not being enough, good enough, pretty enough, and clever enough she sobs like a little girl as though her heart were breaking.

Grant, recognizing this flood of feeling and emotion as genuine, was able to move in and respond in an intuitive and warm loving manner. He moved towards her and took her in his arms, holding her close to him while she sobbed out her hurt. The therapist moved out of the interaction at this moment, allowing their care for each other to take over. One of the strengths of this method is the therapist's deliberate capitalization of the relationship and use of energy between partners, rather than relying on their transferential relationship to the therapist. So instead of using himself, the therapist enabled the regressed partner to receive support from the other partner. The therapist was thus mediating in a process of re-establishing the lost empathy and contact in the partnership.

It had clearly now become imperative for the therapist to facilitate awareness of underlying beliefs about self and other in the relationship (the core interpersonal schema or script beliefs) in order to move the couple forward. These underlying irrational beliefs have kept emerging at various points in the sessions, and are keeping Jessica and Grant locked into non-productive repetitive patterns of interaction. The therapist's recognition and understanding of how embedded beliefs interfere with people's rational well-functioning adult abilities underpins this facilitation process. One of the important aspects of the therapeutic context is this ability to bring these out and work with them so that they stop interfering in people's current lives. The centre of this brief therapeutic approach is the focus on this central disabling dynamic in relationships. The therapist works on the one hand with interactional aspects, while on the other allowing for an in-depth approach by dealing with the intrapsychic issues of each partner. This ends up allowing for an economical, efficient and effective approach to change in individuals and in the system they create by virtue of their interaction.

SESSION 5: DEALING WITH THE UNDERLYING PAIN

Although Jessica had acknowledged the pain and inadequacy she felt at not falling pregnant, it soon emerged that this is a subject that Jessica and Grant avoid talking about except in occasional angry and critical outbursts. Her pain and Grant's grief at his previous losses emerged in this session, creating the opportunity for a deeper level of care and understanding between them. They ceased colluding to avoid the emotional upheaval that this discussion evoked and attended to each other's distress in a loving manner. This session opens up a deeper level of intimacy and sharing between them while at the same time illuminating some of the tensions that have focused on Morgan. From this point onwards they were able to separate their concerns about having a child together from Morgan's needs and his role in their relationship. They both realized that it had been easier to simply argue about Morgan when what they really needed was to face the pain in their own relationship and reach out to one another in an understanding and empathic way.

JESSICA: Since last week's session I have felt so much closer and warmer and better understood by Grant (turns to him). You not only moved towards me but you also helped me a great deal. I kept remembering during the week how warm and thoughtful you were to me in the last session – and you've kept doing that at home. I am very grateful to you both . . . really (with tears in her eyes).

(Couples often wait until the session to fight, but may equally well wait to express love and appreciation. Their tender loving feelings may also embarrass them and they may be as uncertain of how to share these with each other as their angry feelings or their anxieties.)

GRANT: Thank you (to Jessica). I feel quite emotional right now as I remember the image I had of you last week as a sad lonely little girl. I feel angry with your parents for their insensitivity to you . . .

(Therapist cut in and interrupted this process, feeling that it was not going to be too helpful right now to pursue this topic.)

THERAPIST: I wonder if this is a good time to talk about how you two feel about the anxiety and uncertainty created in your lives by the worry of unsuccessfully trying to have a baby?

GRANT: It was on my mind to raise this very issue today, because I realize how much pain I have held back and shut off. You see this situation reminds me of how much I suffered all those years with Melody and never talked about. What I keep forgetting Jessica is how different you are to Melody and how much easier it is for us to talk. We can really face difficulties and problems as they arise . . . but I sometimes forget that. Melody would just get hysterical, weep and scream, and that was the end of any discussion. So . . . I never felt soft towards her as I do with you . . .

THERAPIST (focusing on the blocked feelings and Grant's repressed memories, since Grant is still very emotionally controlled as he said this):   So Grant, what was it like for you when you and Melody kept trying for a baby . . .

GRANT: Well, we were kids really and I suppose unused to any frustrations and difficulties. I would get so angry, but was scared to say anything at the same time. Also Melody got all the fussing and sympathy; no-one really thought I was suffering too. I also kept worrying that it may really be my fault in some way, although of course the doctors assured me otherwise.

Grant went back to the early days of his first marriage and his tensions and anxieties and struggles in that situation. Jessica listened attentively and empathically. Again the therapist was able to step back out of the interaction and allow their natural concern and care for each other to take over. Even though the therapist said very little at this point in the session, his presence did provide a holding context and psychologically supported and sustained a climate of contact, care and empathic listening between the partners.

Some while later Jessica articulated an obvious statement, which the therapist had understood from early on in this work. He had, however, held back from making this interpretation, knowing that if the couple reached this insight themselves it would be far more relevant and meaningful to them.

JESSICA: I guess it has been much easier for us to keep arguing about Morgan and his well-being than for us to really dig into how frightening and upsetting it is to talk about our struggle to have a baby! I keep not wanting to raise the issue because I feel so upset and inadequate . . . as though there is something else I should be doing differently. But I can see that for you Grant it is not only us in the present but also all the memories of the past with Melody. I am so sorry . . .

GRANT (interrupting while at the same time visibly moved):   Yes, and I was scared that you could become like Melody . . . and get hysterical and selfish . . . and at the same time I didn't want to cause you any more pain.

THERAPIST (gently moving the process forward):   And for you, Jessica?

JESSICA: For me . . . I just keep feeling 'not good enough' again . . . that I must be letting Grant down. All over again, and that maybe he should never have married me. I'm also such a control freak that I couldn't bear the feeling of not being able to solve the problem and having it out of my control in this way. I guess I'm sad and angry . . . all at the same time.

GRANT: I think what we need is a stress-free, baby-free and actually Morgan-free holiday. We need to go away together, just you and I and forget about the temperature charts, time of the month, pregnancies, Morgan, Melody . . . and just enjoy ourselves like we did when we first met. You know we never really went on a proper honeymoon – what with the demands from our families . . . and since then we haven't had much alone time. I guess (looking thoughtful) I've felt so guilty about Morgan and the break-up of the marriage that I keep trying to make it up to him. That's really not very fair to you at all. I'm sorry darling. I can be very selfish and unthinking.

THERAPIST (smiling but pushing on with the process):   That sounds like a wonderful idea and I think for today we should still take the opportunity and space to clear up any left-over cobwebs, resentments, misunderstandings.

The therapist was making sure that the couple had not jumped prematurely to closure and too easy an ending, a 'flight into health', while still avoiding something else.

SESSION 6: REVIEW: DEALING WITH FEELINGS

THERAPIST: This is our sixth session together and it is important for us to review what we have achieved in our work together and decide what remains to be done. Perhaps we can begin by each of you taking a turn to reflect on what you have gained in the previous sessions. Then we can focus on what you still want to deal with in the remaining two sessions.

JESSICA: Sure.

GRANT: Yes, I like that suggestion.

JESSICA: I would like to start by saying that the last session was one of the most significant experiences in my relationship with Grant. I am pleased that I was able to talk to you Grant without a quarrel about my sadness at not falling pregnant. I never realized quite how hard it was for you when your first wife miscarried; somehow the fact that you had Morgan seemed to make up for the other losses in my mind. Now I understand better. And it was great to sort things out about Morgan.

GRANT: I feel I have found you again, Jessica.

THERAPIST: I appreciate the courage and honesty that you have both shown in sharing your deepest vulnerabilities. You have been open to exploring the ways in which your communication gets stuck, and I think you both see a clearer way forward. In our final sessions together, we can deal with any remaining issues, review your contracts for the future and take the opportunity to say goodbye to one another.

(Again the therapist pauses and leaves the space for the couple to raise any as yet unspoken issues.)

JESSICA: I know this sounds silly, but Grant I still feel very responsible and very criticized by you at times. You get that disapproving expression on your face and you seem to turn away from me . . . you don't respond to what I'm saying to you. It reminds me so much of my father . . . I used to get so scared of him as a little girl . . .

The therapist resisted the temptation to go back to Jessica's own early beliefs and turned to Grant, who was visibly more relaxed and open. Grant was able to hear and respond to Jessica in an undefensive way. A goal of this brief therapy is for the couple to establish an open way of relating without the therapist's intervention. By this stage in the treatment process the therapist felt optimistic that this couple were in fact well on the road towards managing without him.

GRANT: I guess I get like that when I feel angry and then I don't know what to do . . . so I withdraw into myself. Because there never was a good way of getting angry at home. I think I'm not really dealing with you in that moment Jessica but with my own childhood experience.

JESSICA: Yes that's what it feels like . . . as if you're not really seeing me.

GRANT: My sister and brother and I were always squabbling . . . and Mum and Dad took their side . . . so I don't expect to be taken seriously. But I know you do respect me and understand me.

(This realization on Grant's part felt like another important insight and awareness to the therapist.)

THERAPIST: Jessica, how would it be for you if Grant said directly: 'I feel really angry (irritated/frustrated) right now and what I want is . . .' You see normal anger is simply problem-solving and underlying it there is usually the desire or wish for something to change or something else to happen.

Explanations about feelings, hints on how to express them, and what they mean are very helpful to clients. Anger is a particularly problematic affect and many people struggle with how to constructively express it. There are not many cultural models that are helpful in this regard so that 'rules for rows' and 'handy household hints for fair fighting' are useful and important.

The session continued with further contracting on both sides about the clear and open expression of anger and hurt without 'dumping' on the other person. The therapist reminded Jessica and Grant at the end of the session that they would spend the next session on a review and contracts for the future.

SESSION 7: CONTRACTS FOR THE FUTURE

JESSICA: I am worried about the future . . . I don't know if we are going to manage without therapy. (To the therapist) You've helped us so much and I'm not sure we won't slip back once we finish with you.

THERAPIST: That's why it is important to spend this time to ensure that you can continue to use what you have learnt here. So let's look at agreements for the future.

GRANT: I have given some thought to our contracts for the future of our relationship. I really liked that idea of 'emotional literacy' we talked about; I would like us to continue with our agreement to share our resentments as they come up rather than holding on to them and dumping them weeks or months later. I know I have been as guilty of this as you have, Jessica. And I also want the other part of that agreement – it was great hearing your appreciations after the resentments.

JESSICA: Let me first say my part and then (to therapist) perhaps you can oversee our negotiations! That all sounds very reasonable and grown-up, Grant, but when you get angry you still tend to forget all about our agreements. So I would like us to find a way of flagging up when we approach a danger zone and agree to 'organize a fair fight' that focuses on one issue at a time, as we have learnt to do here.

THERAPIST: You are both clear about what you want to embody in your contracts for the future. Take some time to check what else may be important to consider for the ongoing care of your relationship.

In managing a session of this nature it is useful to leave space for the couple to reinforce the learnings of the work, their strengths and positive aspects, as well as the danger areas and difficulties that could still arise. Where the brief-term intervention has proved to be a good experience it leaves the door open for them to return with a clear sense of the helpfulness and support that therapy can provide for the relationship. This brief-term focused intervention functions like a crisis intervention in that the opportunity for growth and development is very strong. The crisis that causes the couple to seek help already loosens existing defences and ways of coping and so releases energy for change. The importance of leaving them with a positive experience is emphasized.

SESSION 8: LAST SESSION: CLOSURE

THERAPIST: As we come to the end of our time together, let us briefly review what each of you has learnt in the therapy. Then you can firm up your agreements about where you go from here.

GRANT (quickly jumping in):   This has been an enormously enriching and important experience for me. Before I thank you (turning to the therapist) I want to acknowledge how much I appreciate your openness and willingness to engage in this with me and Jessica. In fact, if it hadn't been for how open and persistent you have been – I would not have stayed the course. Now for what I have gained . . . I think the most important thing has been how important it is to express feelings directly and to deal with problems as they come up. All that resentment I collected over the years and the frustration just destroyed any positive feelings I had for Melody – all that was left on both sides was bitterness and anger, and lots of hurt. With you, Jessica, it's been different from the start, but I was beginning to think recently that we could go the same way. I want to make sure that doesn't happen. And for a start, let's spend more time together . . .

JESSICA: That I really want too . . . more time together alone. I also think we should have family conferences, say once a week, where we all three – me you and Morgan – check in with one another and take time to really chat about things. For myself, I'm still amazed at how important my early childhood was and how some of those circumstances still influence me now. But thanks to you (turning to therapist) I have a much better handle on things and I won't get hooked into playing victim so easily. When I do I want you (turning to Grant) to help me snap out of it without putting me down!

GRANT (smilingly): So what can I say, Jessica, that you won't hear as a criticism or put down?

JESSICA: I guess to remind me in the tone of voice you're using now that I'm getting stuck in a 'victimy' place.

GRANT: Sure, I'll give that a go. And if I start getting angry and not saying anything, it will help if you just ask me what I'm angry about.

The couple continued negotiating these changes they want to make, in both the interactions and communication with each other and also in some of the ways they run their lives and form their reconstructed family.

They then reiterated their gratitude to the therapist who ended the session with:

THERAPIST: It has really been a pleasure to work with both of you. I have found you courageous and honest and I respect the way you are both dealing with a situation which isn't as straightforward as it could seem.

(The therapist's real liking and respect for the pair comes through in these words. As we have already stated, respect is crucial in terms of a countertransference response; where it goes with genuine liking and warmth for the clients, so much the better.)

THERAPIST: And remember, life is full of surprises so if you two need a safe place to sort something out, I will always be glad to see you for another agreed time.

Here the therapist had a sense that unless something really untoward happens, it's unlikely that they would need another series of sessions. They might, however, from time to time need a place to resolve or sort out an issue, perhaps to do with Morgan or another family pressure.

In this case, the therapist felt well satisfied with the results of the brief intervention. He smiled to himself as they left the consulting room. It occurred to him that during a relaxed and carefree holiday there was a good chance that an 'unplanned' pregnancy could happen, giving them the baby they both wished for and bringing fulfilment to an already enriched relationship.

If this appears an optimistic outcome, there are indeed many of these in brief therapy. Although relatively healthy and capable, Grant and Jessica were already becoming alienated and escalating the fights between them. Furthermore Morgan could well have manipulated both of them and at the same time become a victim of their tensions.

As we have already indicated in the text, the goal is not necessarily 'happily ever after' but rather problem-resolution focused on the goal of addressing the underlying unresolved issues. In this case the treatment focused on the baggage Grant carried from his first marriage rather than on his childhood legacy. Jessica's early issues were more pertinent to their interaction and to her current situation. However, neither of them had suffered from severe childhood trauma or neglect. Even in cases of more severe early damage, however, the possibility remains for doing powerful therapy and impacting those damaging frames of reference which affect people's relationship lives.

Inevitably we have been able to give only samples of the work done with Jessica and Grant so that the reader has had to fill in the intervening sections. We trust however that we have conveyed enough of the flavour of this work so that interested clinicians can incorporate our model into their existing practice.

13

SUPERVISION OF BRIEF THERAPY WITH COUPLES

Supervision of brief therapy with couples makes special demands on the supervisor. The brevity of the intervention must not be taken as evidence that this work requires only a brief training. In our experience such brief-term therapy requires a background of knowledge and clinical experience to draw upon that may have taken many years to acquire. The ability to assess rapidly and efficiently, the possession of a wide range of interventions and a depth of conceptual knowledge may mean that the most effective brief-term couples therapists are very experienced clinicians. We shall now discuss some issues we consider central to the supervision of brief therapy with couples.

REMAINING FOCUSED ON GOALS AND CONTRACTS

In the supervision of brief therapy with couples the most frequent issue encountered by the therapist is the difficulty of both making specific workable contracts for the work and of remaining focused on the agreed goals. This requirement challenges the therapist's capacity for self-restraint. He needs to stay within the contractual boundaries agreed at the outset and not impose on the clients his own agenda for change. In the initial assessment process, the therapist is often aware of many areas that could be the focus for therapy and that would be of concern to him in his own relationships. However, he needs to be sensitive to the needs of the particular couple and not pressurize them, however subtly, into doing what he thinks is required.

To be viable the contract for the brief therapy needs to emerge from an exploration of the couple's presenting issues and their view of the changes desired in the relationship. Both the process level (an understanding of the central non-productive cycle of reinforcement or 'vicious cycle') and particular content areas will be addressed in the contract. ('We want to learn how to make joint decisions that we both support, without pointless fighting, especially with regard to the parenting of our children from previous marriages').

Supervision provides the therapist with the opportunity to air his observations about the couple's process, to receive appreciation for his insights and to discuss the related theory. In this way, he can extend his thinking and enjoy the exploration of the couple's dynamics in the supervisory context to enhance his work with them and to extend his own knowledge of this field of endeavour. Such an extended exploration may then free him up intellectually and emotionally to focus back on the contract in the work with the particular couple. Supervision can supply this supportive function which will free the therapist to focus effectively in his work with clients. Supervision also provides in this way for the development of the thinking and learning of the therapist, which concerns the supervisor as closely as the interests of the clients, since we believe these two processes bear an intimate relationship to one another. We consider that it is vital that the brief therapy contract can be viewed within a wider relational and developmental perspective, so that the accumulated wisdom, experience and research in the field can inform the therapist in his work. However, once this has been done, the therapist will need to focus back on the agreed contract/s and consider how the information at his disposal can best be used to inform his interventions into the couple's system. There will be a constant interplay in supervision between the processes of extending the therapist's knowledge of the field, and assisting him in refocusing this on his specific work with the clients under review in an effective and economical manner.

In this regard, agreeing contracts that have specific observable behavioural correlates presents a particular challenge to the beginning brief-term couples therapist. One such beginner was puzzled that he was 'stuck' with a couple despite the high level of their motivation. The contract he had agreed with them was worded as follows: 'We will try hard to fight less and attempt to become closer'. On reflection it became clear to the therapist in supervision that the partners were indeed 'trying' but their efforts were simply proving to them and the therapist that the situation was hopeless. They had committed themselves to 'trying to change' but seemingly not to 'succeeding' in the process. When the therapist returned to the next session with this insight, he was able to address this covert dynamic built into the contract with the couple. His explorations revealed that their agreed contract covered a deep-seated despair about the relationship and a fear that nothing could ever change between them. Once these feelings were out in the open and acknowledged by both therapist and clients alike, they agreed a contract to explore their feelings and attitudes about the relationship and whether they wished to pursue it, before agreeing further contracts that took for granted their continuing together. We advise therapists to check out carefully with the couple whether the contract clearly reflects their needs, whether they can 'own it' and identify with it, and how they will each 'know' that the contract is being met by self and other. Such checking will often reveal the existence of embedded 'shoulds' or potential points of sabotage, which may be related to underlying fears or resentments. Clearly these will need to be addressed before moving on or may of themselves provide the contractual focus.

DEALING WITH TRANSFERENCE IN BRIEF THERAPY WITH COUPLES

Dealing with the emergence of transferential feelings on the part of the clients is another issue frequently presented in supervision. The therapist's task is essentially that of a facilitator or mediator in the couple's process, so that she can enable the partners to communicate more effectively without drawing too much of the emotional energy from the relationship onto herself. This requires a stance which balances the acknowledgement of the transference with minimizing the extent to which the therapist directly draws this emotional charge from the participants. In supervision the therapist may explore how to talk openly and directly about projections on to her in such a way that these can be recognized, placed in the appropriate context and the relationship between the partners remain the primary focus for the work. We realize in our own work and in supervising the work of others, that some degree of idealizing transference may be inevitable in this type of therapy. It often happens that the couple begin to idealize the therapist and see that person as 'having all the answers' and 'knowing just how to maintain a relationship'. In supervision, the therapist will explore options for gently confronting these idealizing comments and give the partners the space to express the feelings that underlie them. In one such case, it emerged in the subsequent session that the partners were feeling discouraged because of the anger they were both carrying from the past and which they believed that 'other people' (especially the therapist) could let go of without much effort. In similar vein, the therapist may become the focus of a couple's disappointment or anger that she is not able to 'make it right for them'. This problem when explored in supervision led the therapist to review with the clients their expectations of her, themselves and of each of their respective roles in the change process. In this way, their secret wish that a miracle would occur through their mere attendance at sessions was discussed openly and revealed as an adult derivative of the childhood magical fantasy of a rescuer or 'fairy godmother' who sets all to rights. This process then left the way open for a realistic therapeutic contract related to achievable goals.

DEALING WITH THERAPIST COUNTERTRANSFERENCE IN SUPERVISION

Therapists engaged with the demands of brief therapy with couples are constantly faced with their own countertransferential responses to the work. A frequent supervisory focus is dealing with the alternation of deep involvement with a couple and then the need for disengagement within the short time focus of this type of therapy. This rapid 'in and out' process takes its emotional toll of the therapist. Said by one therapist: 'I feel I have only really begun to know and bond with this couple, and our work together is nearly at an end'; by another: 'I find it really draining to be saying hello and goodbye so often to so many people, and then having no idea of what happens thereafter. I know that's the nature of the work, but it does leave me frustrated at times'. Because the work is emotionally taxing in this way, supervision supplies a contained space where feelings can be aired, heard, supported and normalized so that the therapist is once again open to his work with clients. As supervisors we need to account for the nature of the strain brief therapy places on therapists, especially as effective work of this nature also requires a deep level of engagement by the therapist with the partners and the unit they represent. This is a process that is also faced by medical professionals, but the relational nature of therapeutic work demands that the therapist be fully present to his clients in a way that does not allow for withdrawal behind a professional facade. A therapist's primary tool in his work is the use of self in the therapeutic encounter, with its attendant stresses and rewards, both of which need to be fully recognized.

Another countertransferential issue brought to supervision is the tendency to be drawn into the relationship dynamic of the couple. Therapists are supported to sharpen their awareness of their own responses, sensations and feelings in the sessions. Individual members of a couple may try to triangulate the therapist into the process in an unhelpful or potentially destructive manner. Since much of this process may take place unconsciously, the therapist will need to be alert to signals that he may be invited into a response that will not support the therapeutic goals. Certain feelings on the part of the therapist may be indicators that he is stepping into a projection or that he is allowing personal agenda of his own unrelated to the couple's goals to interfere with the clarity of his thinking. Boredom is often an indicator that personal feelings of the therapist's are being touched upon by the therapy, feelings that he has suppressed and disowned. 'I notice that whenever either of my clients is getting angry, I feel distanced and begin to register boredom.' Undue and excessive curiosity about some aspect of the couple's relationship may relate to unresolved areas in the therapist's own life: 'When he mentioned his admiration of a man's physique, someone he saw in the gym, I found myself asking for all sorts of details that had nothing to do with the discussion.'

These issues can be explored in supervision to separate out the therapist's own unresolved feelings or personal dilemmas from the couple's issues. The therapist's own issues of shame around certain needs and feelings may lead her to keep these hidden in a way that covertly affects the therapy. She may, for instance, avoid any expressions of fear or vulnerability, because of the shame that was induced in her as a child by any sign of these natural responses. In this sense, she may then be colluding with her clients to prevent their exposure to similar humiliation, thus actually supporting them in the avoidance of tender emotions. Sometimes, the therapist will contract to explore a personal issue further in his own personal therapy, particularly if this arises more than once in supervision in relation to his client work. Any countertransferential pattern may require deeper work than appropriate in a supervisory analysis of the situation.

We have mentioned previously that a regular challenge for the couples therapist comes from an invitation to be the 'referee' or the 'judge' in the couple's interaction, where the wish is that he will decide who is in the right and who is in the wrong. If the therapist is triangulated into the process in this way, he will almost certainly lose the respect of both partners in the long run, even if one person is momentarily pleased with being exonerated from blame. A particular challenge for one of the writers arose when supervising a therapist who was dealing with a couple where one partner, Frank, was a member of the legal profession. Frank could not understand why the therapist was not prepared to take up the role of 'judge' or arbiter of the relationship: 'After all, you are the expert in marriage and communication, surely you can tell who is right around here'. Frank even brought a long written deposition to one of the sessions which he called 'the case for the prosecution' and invited his partner Susan to prepare her 'defence'. In supervision the therapist was supported to go back to the next session and clarify his role as a facilitator and mediator: 'In my view you are both right about how you see things. The challenge is not in deciding who is right and who is wrong, but in getting you to understand one another's views and respect that difference'. Finally Frank conceded that his legal framework might not be equally useful or relevant to his intimate relationship. He was able to recognize that proving the other to be at fault might not lead to greater intimacy but only to the satisfaction of being 'right'. From that point onwards, the therapist was able to agree a contract with the couple (a concept Frank had no difficulty in accepting) and proceed with the joint work.

LEARNING TO USE HOMEWORK ASSIGNMENTS IN BRIEF THERAPY WITH COUPLES

Brief therapy with couples can be enhanced and supported by homework assignments where these grow out of the sessions and are directly related to the agreed goals. The advantage of having two clients who are working on a joint endeavour is a particular bonus for the therapist. This means that skills learnt and tested in the therapy can be reinforced at home in between sessions. Suggesting and creating useful homework tasks is a challenge for the beginner in this field. The most effective tasks prove to be those that couples contribute themselves or those suggested by the therapist in a sensitive response to the couple's emerging needs.

However, a word of caution is in place here. Premature or misplaced or unthought-through tasks can do more damage than none at all. To suggest that a couple share all their accumulated resentments towards one another before the next session may be well meant, but is almost guaranteed to be destructive. Such a task would be better attempted in one or more therapy sessions where the therapist can ensure that the process stays clear. Homework tasks need to be carefully graded to suit the level of interaction of a couple. Such tasks will evoke some anxiety, but if this is too high, the couple may avoid the task altogether or do it once and end up in a fight that sets them back and undermines their faith in the effectiveness of therapy. Supervision provides a place where the grading of tasks/experiments can be evaluated and carefully planned. For example, a couple who were not talking to one another beyond the bare civilities required by everyday living agreed to a homework task that involved them in sitting down together for half an hour each day and taking turns to share what they had done that day. The listener's task was simply to attend and indicate that he/she understood and followed the storyline. This basic task enabled the couple gradually to open up their communication again, starting in this 'non-threatening' way until they built up to more intimate exchanges. If they had been asked to start with the expression of their feelings for one another, the supervisor's prediction was that they would either not complete the task or become caught up in their characteristic 'vicious cycle' of interaction.

THERAPIST QUALITIES AND THERAPIST'S USE OF SELF

The model of brief therapy we have outlined in this book calls for robustness and flexibility on the part of the therapist. The requirements of this type of work are taxing and demanding in every way. The therapist needs to deal robustly with the circumscribed nature of the work and keep himself focused on the agreed goals. A tendency to be manipulated and attracted into associated pathways that take him away from the central focus can easily undermine the effectiveness of his work. In addition, this approach calls for flexibility on the part of the therapist, who needs to be available as a model to the clients whilst at the same time employing a wide range of interventions in order to complete his task in the allotted time. The discipline required to keep task-focused may not suit all temperaments.

We have stressed the impact on the therapist of the process of intense engagement and disengagement within a relatively short time period. The challenge of this emotionally demanding process is heightened by the fact that in a relationship model of therapy, the therapist's use of self is a primary medium for change in the clients. Although the therapist will work to clearly defined goals and specified contracts, it is the therapist as person that may prove an important role model for the partners. Open clear communication, compassion for the pain of others combined with interpersonal robustness and the ability to listen in a non-judgmental, accepting manner that undoes the shame-binds of the past characterize the therapists who are attracted to this type of work. To this may also be added a certain pragmatism about achievable and measurable goals in the work of their choice and a capacity for dealing effectively with the many and frequent endings involved in brief therapy.

ADDRESSING ISSUES OF POWER IN SUPERVISION

Supervision provides the opportunity to address the nature and exercise of power in the therapeutic relationship. In this regard we find helpful French and Raven's classification of power (quoted in Holloway, 1995) which has been applied to supervisors but can easily be seen as relevant to therapists likewise. This classification lists different types of power which can be summarized as follows. Reward power we invest in people we perceive as being able to mediate sources of reward and gratification; coercive power we attribute to people whom we perceive as mediating punishment; legitimate power refers to a person's perceived power as a professionally sanctioned provider of a service; expert power is attributed to a person for their mastery of knowledge and skills; and finally, referent power derives from interpersonal attractiveness (French and Raven in Holloway 1995, p. 32). This classification can serve as the basis for supervisory reflections on the effects of power of different kinds in brief therapy with couples.

The therapist is usually perceived as possessing reward and coercive power, no matter how neutral and non-judgmental the stance that she takes up, because of projections that derive from people's past experience of those in authority positions. For this reason, the therapist may need to take the initiative to bring this issue into the open, so that her attitudes can be challenged by the partners, particularly at points where they experience a bias on her part. If this material can be openly addressed, the likelihood of misunderstanding and the misuse of power will be reduced. Supervision provides the opportunity for the therapist to examine any tendencies she may be feeling to 'reward' one partner at the expense of 'punishing' the behaviour of the other. The containment provided by the contractual focus of brief therapy with couples can support a clear uncontaminated process in this regard. The therapist's legitimate power rests in the profession of psychotherapy. In supervision, ethical and professional codes of practice are regularly in focus, as therapists deal with boundary issues or their relationships with their professional peers. We have also found supervision provides a context for evaluating a therapist's expert power and the impact this may have on the couple. It is inevitable in the profession of psychotherapy that therapists' reputations will be a matter for discussion and enquiry amongst prospective clients. Sometimes therapists have felt that the expert power vested in them by prospective clients is not warranted by their actual ability and level of training. Such expectations can be carefully checked out and evaluated with the supervisor, who has intimate and unbiased knowledge of the therapist's work built up over a period of time. Sometimes the supervisory challenge is to assist a therapist in owning their mastery of their therapeutic work, where the person tends to undervalue their own expertise. Most difficult of all for many people in this culture is acknowledging that they possess interpersonal attractiveness that may well draw people to them. Not accounting for this dimension of power (or for some the over-rating of it), may well lead a therapist to ignore or be unaware of certain vital features of her interaction with a couple. Said by one therapist: 'My aim as a therapist is to have presence, not to possess charisma!'

Because of these different levels and kinds of power invested in the therapist, it is vital for the therapist to be aware of any tendency on her part to take advantage of the vulnerability and dependency of the people in her care. The therapist can use supervision to address her own unresolved issues about power and authority as these impact on her work with clients. A regular review with the supervisor of her work with all her clients is essential even where she feels confident of her work with a particular couple. As an unbiased and uninvolved outsider, the supervisor can be on the alert for any signs that the therapist's own issues about authority and control may be clouding her judgment. Over-involvement is often the first indicator that all is not well in the power balance in a particular therapist–client relationship. This can be immediately and thoroughly investigated in the supervisory context and any remedial action taken promptly.

This is a challenging field for both the therapist and the supervisor. It is encouraging for the authors that couples appear to be seeking help much earlier in their relationships so that an effective brief intervention can often avert years of slow erosion and give the couple support at a point before disillusionment has set in or there is so much accumulated resentment that repair is impossible or constitutes a painful long-term process.

REFERENCES AND
BIBLIOGRAPHY

Bader, E. & Pearson, P.T. (1988). *In Quest of the Mythical Mate*. New York: Brunner/Mazel.

Beitman, B.D. (1992). Integration through fundamental similarities and useful differences among the schools. In J.C. Norcross and M.R. Goldfried (Eds), *Handbook of Psychotherapy Integration*, New York: Basic Books, pp. 202–230.

Berne, E. (1961). *Transactional Analysis in Psychotherapy*, New York: Ballantine Books.

Berne, E. (1963). *The Structures and Dynamics of Organisations and Groups*, New York: Grove Press.

Berne, E. (1964). *Games People Play*, London: Penguin Books.

Berne, E. (1966). *Principles of Group Treatment*. San Francisco: Shea Books.

Boyd, L.W. & Boyd, H.S. (1981). A transactional model for relationship counseling. *Transactional Analysis Journal*, **11** (2), 142–146.

Brown, T. & Landrum-Brown, J. (1995). Counselor supervision: cross-cultural perspectives. In J.G. Ponterotto, J.M. Casas, L.A. Suzuki, C.M. Alexander (Eds), *Handbook of Multicultural Counseling*, London: Sage Publications, pp. 263–286.

Buber, M. (1994). *I and Thou*, (trans. W. Kaufman), Edinburgh: T & T Clark (first published 1923).

Clark, B. (1991). Empathic transactions in the deconfusion of child ego States. *Transactional Analysis Journal*, **21** (2), 92–97.

Delisle, G. (1988). *Balises II: A Gestalt Perspective of Personality Disorders*, Montreal: Le Centre D'Intervention Gestaltiste, Le Reflet.

Dicks, H.V. (1993). *Marital Tensions*, London: Karnac Books (first published 1967).

Erikson, E.H. (1950). *Childhood and Society*, London: Penguin Books (first published in 1950).

Erskine, R.G. (1982). Transactional analysis and family therapy. In A.M. Horne & M.M. Ohlsen (Eds), *Family Counseling and Therapy*, Itasca, IL: F.E. Peacock, pp. 245–275.

Erskine, R.G. & Zalcman, M.J. (1979). The racket system. *Transactional Analysis Journal*, **9** (1), 92–97.

Goldfried, M. (1995). Toward a common language for case formulation. *Journal of Psychotherapy Integration*, **5** (3), 221–244, New York: Plenum.

Greenspan, R.R. (1965). The working alliance and transference neuroses. *Psychoanalysis Quarterly*, **34**, 155–181.

Hall, A.D. & Fagin, R.E. (1956). Definition of system. In *General Systems Yearbook*, Vol. 1, pp. 18–28.

Holloway, E. (1995). *Clinical Supervision: A Systems Approach*, London: Sage.

Hycner, R. (1993). *Between Person and Person*, New York: The Gestalt Journal Press.

Jaffe, S.S. & Viertal, J. (1979). *Becoming Parents: Preparing for the Emotional Changes of First Time Parenthood*, New York: Athenaeum.

Kahn, E., Rogers, C. & Kohut, H. (1989). *On the Importance of Valuing the Self: Self Psychology: Comparisons & Contrasts*, Hillsdale, NJ: Analytic Press.

Karpman, S. (1968). Fairy tales and script drama analysis. *Transactional Analysis Bulletin*: Selected Articles from Volumes 1–9, 1976, San Francisco, TA Press, pp. 51–56.

Karpman, S. (1971). Options, *Transactional Analysis Journal*, **1** (1), 79–87.

Kaufman, G. (1993). *The Psychology of Shame*, London: Routledge.

Lifton, J. (1993). From Hiroshima to the Nazi doctors: the evolution of psychoformative approaches to understanding traumatic stress syndromes. In J. Wilson and B. Raphael (Eds) *International Handbook of Traumatic Stress Syndromes*, New York: Plenum.

Mahler, M.S., Pine, F. & Bergman, A. (1975). *The Psychological Birth of the Human Infant*, New York: Basic Books.

Maslow, A.H. (1970). *Motivation and Personality*, (2nd edn). New York: Harper and Row.

Morris, W. (ed.) (1981). *Arnenden Heritage Dictionary of the English Language*, Boston: Houghton Mifflin.

Nathanson, D.L. (1992). *Shame and Pride*, New York: Norton.

Ogen, T.H. (1982). *Projective Identification and Psychotherapeutic Technique*. New York: Aronson.

Polster, E. (1995). *A Population of Selves*, San Francisco: Jossey-Bass.

Rogers, C.R. (1951). *Client-Centered Therapy*, Boston, MA: Houghton Mifflin.

Ryle, A. (1992). *Cognitive-Analytic Therapy: Active Participation in Change*, Chichester: Wiley.

Schiff, J.L. et al. (1975). *Cathexis Reader: Transactional Analysis Treatment of Psychosis*, New York: Harper & Row.

Solomon, M.F. (1992). *Narcissism and Intimacy: Love and Marriage in an Age of Confusion*, New York: Norton.

Steiner, C.M. (1984). Emotional literacy. *Transactional Analysis Journal*, 14 (3), 162–173.

Sterba, R. (1934). The face of the ego in analytic therapy, *International Journal of Psychoanalysis*, **15** 117–126.

Stern, D. (1985). *The Interpersonal World of the Infant*, New York: Basic Books.

Stevens, J.O. (1971). *Awareness*, London: Eden Grove.

Stolorow, R.D. & Atwood, G.E. (1992). *Contexts of Being: The Intersubjective Foundations of Psychological Life*, London: The Analytic Press.

Stolorow, R.D., Atwood, G.E. & Brandschaft, B. (Eds) (1994). *The Intersubjective Perspective*, London: Jason Aronson.

Sullivan, H.S. (1953). *The Interpersonal Theory of Psychiatry*, New York: Norton.

Watzlawick, P., Weakland, J. and Fisch, R. (1974). *Change*, New York: Norton.

Weiss, E. (1950). *Principles of Psychodynamics*, New York: Grune & Stratton.

Wheeler, G. (1991). *Gestalt Reconsidered*, Gestalt Institute of Cleveland Press, New York: Gardner Press.

Wheeler, G. & Backman, S. (Eds) (1994). *On Intimate Ground*, San Francisco: Jossey-Bass.

Wile, D.B. (1981). *Couples Therapy: A Nontraditional Approach*, New York: Wiley.

Winnicott, D.W. (1971). Transitional objects and transitional phenomena. In *Playing and Reality*, London: Tavistock/Routledge.

Winnicott, D.W. (1989). In Clare Winnicott, Ray Shepherd, Madeleine Davis (Eds), *Psycho-Analytic Explorations*, London: Karnac Books.

Yontef, G.M. (1993). *Awareness, Dialogue and Process*, New York: Gestalt Journal Press.

Zeigarnik, B. (1927). Das Behalten erledigter und unerledigter Handlungen. *Psychologische Forschungen*, **9**, 1–85.

INDEX

Related titles of interest from Wiley...

Brief Therapeutic Consultations
An Approach to Systemic Counselling
Eddy Street and Jim Downey

Provides a practical framework which describes how to construct a client-counsellor relationship which is brief, collaborative and consultative in purpose but therapeutic in form.

Wiley Series in Brief Therapy & Counselling
0-471-96343-7 160pp 1996 Paperback

Brief Rational Emotive Behaviour Therapy
Windy Dryden

This book represents a response to the growing need for brief, time-limited methods for counselling and therapy.

Wiley Series in Brief Therapy & Counselling
0-471-95786-0   244pp   1995   Paperback

Intensive Short-Term Dynamic Psychotherapy
Theory and Technique
Patricia Della Selva

Illustrates that ambitious therapeutic goals, including character change, are possible within a brief period of approximately 40 sessions.

0-471-04717-1   272pp   1995   Hardback

Brief Psychotherapy
CMT: An Integrative Approach in Clinical Practice
Francis Macnab

0-471-94078-X   342pp 1993 Paperback

International Journal of Short-Term Psychotherapy
Editors: **Tewfik Said** and **J-M. Gaillard**
0884-724X